P9-BYZ-993

NOW I KNOW

THE
SOVIETS
INVADED
WISCONSIN?!

...And 99 More Interesting Facts,
PLUS THE AMAZING
STORIES BEHIND THEM

Pirates Wrecked
the Metric System

Potatoes Beat a
Naval Destroyer

Disney Employs
Chickens

You Can't Sell
Your Pee

Football Can
Save Your Life

DAN LEWIS, Author of *Now I Know*

Adams Media
New York London Toronto Sydney New Delhi

DEDICATION

To Stephanie, Ethan, Alex, Annie, and my parents.

A adams media

Adams Media
An Imprint of Simon & Schuster, Inc.
57 Littlefield Street
Avon, Massachusetts 02322

Copyright © 2019 by Dan Lewis.

All rights reserved, including the right to reproduce this book or portions thereof in any form whatsoever. For information address Adams Media Subsidiary Rights Department, 1230 Avenue of the Americas, New York, NY 10020.

First Adams Media hardcover edition October 2019

ADAMS MEDIA and colophon are trademarks of Simon & Schuster.

For information about special discounts for bulk purchases, please contact Simon & Schuster Special Sales at 1-866-506-1949 or business@simonandschuster.com.

The Simon & Schuster Speakers Bureau can bring authors to your live event. For more information or to book an event contact the Simon & Schuster Speakers Bureau at 1-866-248-3049 or visit our website at www.simonspeakers.com.

Interior design by Julia Jacintho
Interior images © 123RF; Clipart.com

Manufactured in the United States of America

10 9 8 7 6 5 4 3 2 1

Library of Congress Cataloging-in-Publication Data has been applied for.

ISBN 978-1-5072-1015-4
ISBN 978-1-5072-1016-1 (ebook)

Many of the designations used by manufacturers and sellers to distinguish their products are claimed as trademarks. Where those designations appear in this book and Simon & Schuster, Inc., was aware of a trademark claim, the designations have been printed with initial capital letters.

CONTENTS

INTRODUCTION

Are You Curious?

I'm curious. I like to learn about the world. And I like to share the stories I discover along the way. That's why I first started "Now I Know"—then as an email newsletter—in the summer of 2010. The satisfaction you get from learning something new—something that you even doubt at first because it's just too strange (like Soviets invading Wisconsin)—is truly addicting. So I can't tell you how happy I am that your curiosity has led you to this book.

In *Now I Know: The Soviets Invaded Wisconsin?!* I've collected one hundred of my favorite fascinating facts and the stories behind them. You'll learn about the time McDonald's tried to trick kids into eating more broccoli. (Hint: It involved bubblegum.) You'll find out about the fateful day during World War II when the Americans and the Germans actually teamed up. You'll even read about why it may be okay to let a perfect stranger stick something in your ear—if you're in Chengdu, at least. And yes, you'll also learn about the time when a small Wisconsin town was overrun by Communists (kind of).

Each story connects to the last in some way, because while I don't expect you to read this entire book in a day, I hope that each piece of mind-boggling trivia you do read inspires you to learn more. Each fact also comes with a bonus fact, so really, you're getting two hundred incredible facts. And when you're done? There's more. That email newsletter I started years ago is still around today: Just go to NowIKnow.com to sign up for free. You'll get a fun new story to satisfy your curiosity each and every weekday.

With every fascinating story, you'll be able to declare "now I know." So let that curiosity take the lead. Turn the page to find out what the measles have to do with phone numbers, or flip through to any fact that calls to you. The world of the truly bizarre and unbelievable awaits!

THE DIGIT DISEASE

How Measles Led to Phone Numbers

It's your unique identification number. Ten to fifteen digits you regularly give to other people without much of a second thought, even those you've just met and, in some cases, have never spoken to before. It's your phone number!

Phone numbers have been around since 1880 and are an integral part of the modern communication infrastructure. But when phone networks were originally developed, there wasn't an immediate need for phone numbers. You'd simply pick up the receiver and be connected with an operator who would connect you to any person or business you needed to contact. And because calls in those days were local and the operators were local too, callers were usually connected correctly and quickly.

Telephone numbers probably didn't even cross the minds of those in charge of phone companies in those days. One of the first-ever phone books, for example, didn't use numbers at all; published in New Haven, Connecticut, it simply listed the handful of businesses in the area that had phones. The entire "book" fit on one single page; why bother developing a numbering system to accommodate fewer than one hundred customers?

However, in 1879, something happened in Lowell, Massachusetts, that changed phone history forever. In this year, Lowell found itself home to two things: a new telephone switchboard and a measles epidemic. Now the idea that the measles would have any effect on telephone operations seems strange, but in the time of manual switchboards and no vaccinations for disease, the measles put the entire system at risk.

The Lowell system was staffed by four people, and each ran the risk of contracting the disease. If the Lowell switchboard lost its operators, how would they connect calls? Backup switchboard operators were an option, but they didn't know the switchboard as well as the regular employees, so calls might not have been connected as quickly or accurately.

A physician named Moses Greeley Parker came up with the solution. The phone company would assign a unique ID number to each of its customers (roughly two hundred total), corresponding with each customer's location on the internal switchboard. Now when a caller rang the operator, he or she would provide the ID number of the party the caller was trying to reach. The switchboard operator would have no trouble finding that number on the board in front of him or her, even if he or she had no previous experience as an operator for that community.

Surprisingly, Dr. Parker's suggestion wasn't well received at first. Many customers objected to being reduced to an arbitrary set of digits. According to Ammon Shea, author of *The Phone Book: The Curious History of the Book That Everyone Uses But No One Reads*, many customers expressed that they "would sooner give up their telephones entirely rather than submit themselves to the dehumanizing indignity of being identified by a number." But reason eventually prevailed: When it came to preventing the measles from stopping phone service, Dr. Parker's solution was the best bet the town had. The phone company adopted his solution, and Lowell, Massachusetts, became the first town in the United States with phone numbers.

BONUS FACT

Dial the number, wait for the other side to pick up, and start talking. The phone is a pretty easy tool to use. But that wasn't always the case. Shea, in an interview about his book with *Failure* magazine, noted that "nobody had any idea how to use one....When people first started using the telephone they would often yell into the wrong part." The solution? Early phone books came with instructions for how to use the phone.

AT "WHATEVER" COST

*The Collect Call Campaign You
Wish You Thought Of*

The invention of cell phones changed telecommunications forever. If you look back in time to before their widespread popularity, you'd see a number of things that are either disappearing rapidly at this very minute or no longer exist at all. Pay phones, for example, were once everywhere—on street corners and outside businesses, waiting for you at rest stops along highways. Long-distance phone calls were also priced higher than local ones, and the longer the distance, the longer the per-minute fee.

Perhaps the biggest difference from days before the cell phone were "collect calls." When calling "collect," the *caller* wouldn't pay; instead, the phone company would charge the person *being* called.

For most of the United States' collect call history, business giant AT&T ruled the telecom roost. Not only was AT&T the nation's largest long-distance provider by far—it was also a monopoly in most cases until regulators broke it up in 1982. As the easiest way to make a collect call was to dial zero for the operator, and AT&T was almost always the company for which the operator worked, AT&T became the go-to company when making a collect call. This persisted even after regulators stepped in; when those placing collect calls were asked to choose a long-distance company, the most common answer was "AT&T."

But it wasn't the only answer. Some collect callers were simply indifferent to who provided the long-distance service—the callers themselves weren't footing the bill, after all. In a very honest moment, many of them would simply reply that they didn't care or that it didn't matter.

And to a small company in Texas, that answer proved profitable.

In 1996, *People* magazine shared the story of a Dallas-area company named KTNT Communications. KTNT was one of hundreds of Texas-based companies registered as a long-distance provider for collect calls. If you were a dialer who didn't care which company connected your call, KTNT shouldn't have been at the top of the list: For a three-minute Houston-to-Dallas call, AT&T charged just under $5; for the same call, KTNT charged $7.50. And yet, in many cases, the person you were calling ended up paying KTNT. Why? Because KTNT opened subsidiary companies named "I Don't Know," "It Doesn't Matter," "I Don't Care," and "Whatever."

The operator wouldn't just connect your call using these creatively named subsidiaries, however. KTNT president Dennis Dees told the Associated Press that the practice "was not deceptive at all," as KTNT instructed local telephone companies to inform callers that they were being connected via a company with the same name as their response. The AP tested this claim and found that typically, the operator would verify unprompted that, yes, they wanted to use the company called "I Don't Care" (or whichever company they accidentally chose). As a result, the scheme made KTNT quite a bit money—before the cell phone made collect calls virtually obsolete, at least.

One person who probably didn't make a lot of collect calls? Frank Sinatra. On December 8, 1963, his then nineteen-year-old son, Frank Sinatra Jr., was kidnapped. The kidnappers negotiated a ransom for his release but would only talk to Frank Sr., and only if the latter were using a pay phone. Frank Jr. was ultimately released unharmed (and the criminals were apprehended and convicted), but Frank Sr. carried the memory of the traumatic event with him from that point on, and, wanting to be sure he could use a pay phone whenever necessary, kept ten dimes in his pocket for the rest of his life—and beyond. He is buried with a dollar's worth in dimes.

8-6-7-5-3-0-*MINE*

When Plumbers Battled
over Pop Culture

In 1981, Tommy Tutone came out with the song "867-5309/ Jenny," which took the world by storm. The song is about a phone number written on a bathroom stall, instructing the passerby to call Jenny for a "good time." Jenny, per the song lyrics, could be reached at 867-5309—a number Tutone repeats over a dozen times during the four-minute song.

When the song became a hit—and Tutone's only real success in the music industry—it turned the fictional Jenny's phone number into a real-life target for prank calls. People would call up 867-5309 with their area code, ask for Jenny, laugh, and hang up. And because of this, real people who happened to be reachable at 867-5309 asked their phone companies for a new phone number. Most people, that is. Some decided to capitalize on the opportunity—and sue to protect it.

The story of the battle over 867-5309 begins at Brown University in Providence, Rhode Island, in 1999. The university was given the entire block of phone numbers in the 867 exchange in area code 401, and assigned (401) 867-5309 to a student dormitory (there's also an urban legend floating around that the school specifically assigned two freshman students named Jenny to the room with that number). The students were flooded with prank calls. So, in 2001, the school gave up the number to a regional plumbing company named Gem Plumbing and Heating, who in turn acquired the number in area code 617 (the greater Boston area) as well, which trademarked the number in both regions. If you wanted a plumber in the Boston or Providence areas, you called Gem, not Jenny, but at this well-known phone number.

However, perhaps coincidentally, Gem wasn't the only plumber who saw the obvious tie-in between bathroom stall graffiti and additional business. Florida-based Clockwork Home Services also wanted Jenny's number, and, like Gem, they jumped to claim it. Clockwork, under the name Benjamin Franklin Plumbing, acquired the toll-free number (866) 867-5309 and marked it as "867-5309/Benny." As both numbers worked in Gem's region, Gem sued, asking the court to stop Clockwork from using its trademarked number in the 401 and 617 area codes. According to *USA TODAY*, Gem won the lawsuit.

Since then, though, the two plumbers have apparently figured out a way to get along. In area codes 401 and 617, 867-5309 will give you the corporate offices of Gem. And if you dial 1-866-867-5309 in the Providence, Rhode Island, area? You'll be connected with Benjamin Franklin Plumbing.

BONUS FACT

The real Ben Franklin wasn't a plumber, but he was a lot of other things—including the first Postmaster General of the United States. In fact, his appointment as Postmaster in 1775 predated the nation's official founding. In his honor, the Postal Service operates the B. Free Franklin Post Office in his hometown of Philadelphia. It is designed to reflect postal life in Franklin's era. To stay true to that time period, the Franklin Post Office is the only one in the country that doesn't fly an American flag, as the flag didn't exist back then.

GIVE ME LIBERTY OR GIVE ME CHALUPAS

Taco Bell Pulls the Chain on the Liberty Bell

Public-private partnerships are a long-standing way for corporations to reach consumers while the public coffers find economic relief. Throughout the United States, for example, you'll see signs along different highways noting that a particular company or organization has "adopted" that stretch of road. The benefactor pays for the maintenance of that section (e.g., garbage cleanup) and, in exchange, gets a small sponsorship message that passing drivers will see. While some object to this as part of a larger over-commercialization issue, others see it as an acceptable way to defray the costs of public thoroughfares and attractions.

But in the mid-1990s, however, one company went too far. That company was Taco Bell, and via a full-page ad in seven papers across the country, they announced their purchase of an American landmark: the Liberty Bell.

The Liberty Bell is an artifact from the Revolutionary War period that is located in Philadelphia, Pennsylvania. Legend has it that the bell rang to mark the Second Continental Congress's vote to declare independence from Great Britain on July 2, 1776.

By the mid-1850s, the Liberty Bell had become a symbol of freedom in the United States.

Taco Bell wanted the Liberty Bell to also be a symbol of *financial* freedom, apparently, because, on April 1, 1996, the company blanketed the nation with hundreds of thousands of dollars in newspaper ads announcing their new acquisition. In exchange for a sizable (undisclosed) donation intended to offset America's national debt, Taco Bell had acquired the Liberty Bell. The renamed "Taco Liberty Bell" was to remain in Philadelphia most of the time, but as part of the deal, Taco Bell would relocate it for a few weeks each year to its headquarters in Irvine, California. The company hoped that their efforts would lead to other corporations following in kind—to "do their part," as the ad said, in reducing the national debt.

Many citizens were outraged. Thousands called either the National Park Service or Taco Bell (or both) to voice their negative responses. The National Park Service itself was quite confused about what was going on; a Philadelphia-based spokesperson for the organization told *The Philadelphia Inquirer* that she was caught by surprise herself, only finding out about the decision when she saw the ad in her local newspaper.

Taco Bell's corporate phones were receiving thousands of calls, as were newspaper offices across the country, as Americans tried to figure out how such a thing could happen. However, some people didn't bother to call or complain—they had noticed something significant at the top of the page: the date. It was April 1—April Fools' Day! Taco Bell's ad was a prank; the Liberty Bell was never for sale, and the fast-food chain revealed as much later on that day.

Not everyone was pleased by the joke, but most were good spirited about it. Philadelphia's mayor at the time even joked back at the company, noting that the city was investing $10 million to $15 million in a new pavilion and visitor center for the Taco

Liberty Bell. He invited Taco Bell to pick up the tab (the company passed on this request, but to its credit, had already agreed to donate $50,000 to the bell's maintenance). The White House also got in on the joke; its spokesperson, Mike McCurry, joshed that the nation "will be doing a series of these things. Ford Motor Company is planning an effort to refurbish the Lincoln Memorial. It'll be the Lincoln Mercury Memorial."

BONUS FACT

Programs that allow for the adoption of part of a highway can be quite controversial—just ask the state of Missouri. In 2005, the Ku Klux Klan tried to adopt a section of a highway outside of St. Louis. The state did not want to permit the Klan to do so, but the courts disagreed, requiring that the KKK be treated like any other organization. So the state struck back another way: They renamed the adopted section of highway after Rosa Parks.

THE GREATEST SOCCER PLAYER WHO NEVER WAS

How to Become a Professional Athlete When You Aren't Very Good

Carlos Henrique Raposo, who went by "Carlos Kaiser," was born on April 2, 1963, one day after April Fools' Day. It's too bad, too, because he was a master at playing other people for fools.

A resident of Brazil, Kaiser was born a soccer fan, and like many of his classmates, he played youth soccer as both an adolescent and as a teen. Unlike most of his friends, though, Kaiser's playing caught the eye of a professional club team. In 1979—when he was just sixteen years old—he became the newest member of Puebla. Unfortunately, things didn't work out: Puebla released him before he ever played a game. While he *was* an athletic young man, he wasn't a very good soccer player.

Undeterred, Kaiser decided to try a different career path: a con artist who hid his pedestrian ability by never actually playing in a game. At the time, marginal soccer players could find limited work on short-term contracts that lasted for weeks or months. Kaiser quickly discovered that whatever coaches thought a fill-in soccer player should look like, he looked the part. Some of his professional soccer player friends would even attest to his physical abilities, simply leaving out the part about his lack of soccer skills, which gave him a leg up on the competition. One team after another would sign Kaiser to a short contract.

A guaranteed paycheck in hand, he would then put his plan into action. He'd say he needed a month or so to get back into peak physical shape. Then, he would join the team for practices—and fall shortly after he got onto the pitch, claiming to have pulled a hamstring (and if that didn't work, he had a dentist at the ready to lie about an infection). Without modern techniques available to diagnose the injury, the team would simply keep Kaiser on the bench until his contract ran out.

But that's not what the local press would report. Kaiser took advantage of his access to free team gear, using it to bribe local reporters to write fawning reviews of his soccer prowess. So when Kaiser finally "healed" and was in search of a new team, it was easier to get another contract. From 1979 and into the 1990s, he signed contracts with as many as ten different soccer teams. And he never played in a single game!

There was one close call, however. In the late 1980s, Kaiser signed with the Brazilian team, Bangu. At the time, one of its owners was a man named Castor de Andrade. Castor was a big fan of Kaiser (or the legend of Kaiser, at least) and was getting increasingly frustrated that he wasn't playing. So he forced the issue. Early during one match, with Bangu down 2-0, Castor sent a message to the coach that Kaiser was to be put into the game. Kaiser acted quickly. He spotted an opposing fan in the stands who was heckling the team and, as reported by *The Guardian*, "used it as an excuse to start a brawl with the away supporters." The referees immediately threw Kaiser out of the game—before he had even gotten onto the pitch.

Yet he wasn't thrown off the team for his errant behavior. He told Castor that the fan had accused Castor of being a thief—Kaiser was just defending his honor! Castor, still enamored with the soccer star, not only forgave him but also gave him a six-month contract extension.

BONUS FACT

Outside of the US and Canada, soccer is typically called "football." How did these two very different words come to mean the same thing? The sport (whichever term you prefer) is more formally known as "association soccer," a name coined to differentiate the game from rugby football. The latter's name shortened over time to simply "rugby," making the second use of "football" less confusing. In some areas, however, "association" was shortened—to "soccer." According to the Oxford English Dictionary, "soccer" became its own, stand-alone term in 1863.

BLEEDING PACKER GREEN

*The Lifesaving Powers of Being
an NFL Superfan*

As professional sports teams go, the National Football League's Green Bay Packers have one of the most interesting relationships with their fans. Unlikely most other teams, the Packers are owned by a publicly held nonprofit organization (it's one of the few teams you can buy shares of). This means the team is largely owned by fans. A share of Packers stock isn't easily transferable (there have only been five stock sales windows in the team's nearly one-hundred-year history); if you're one of the roughly 360,000 shareholders, there is a good chance that you or your family has lived in the Green Bay, Wisconsin, area (or maybe you just really love the Packers).

But for a true Packers fan, there's an even higher honor than being part-owner: You may be one of the few people inducted into the team's Fan Hall of Fame. To achieve this honor, it's not enough to go to the games or wear a piece of foam cheese on your head. It takes a dedication that goes above and beyond: You have to truly be a Packers fan in your blood. And blood is actually why, in March 2010, seventy-nine-year-old Jim Becker of Racine,

Wisconsin, became the twelfth fan inducted into the Packers' Fan Hall of Fame.

Becker's induction earned him a bounty of rewards: four high-end seats to a home game; a $500 gift certificate to the fan shop; game tickets, airfare, and accommodations to an away game; and more. But those prizes pale in comparison to what his fandom may have *already* earned him: an extra thirty or more years on his life.

From 1952 until 2008, Becker did something few other fans have done: He attended *every single* Packers home game. The tickets, though, were hardly free, and Becker—a father to eleven kids—had to get creative to make ends meet. He found out that he could sell his blood for $15 per pint, and, at least during the early part of his fifty-five years of attendance, that was more than enough to cover the cost of game entry.

As the 1960s rolled into the 1970s, Becker continued his blood-for-football tradition. And it's probably a good thing he did. Becker's father passed away suddenly at the age of forty-three; as Becker told ABC News, his seemingly healthy dad got sick one day and then, three days later, "his organs failed." The cause of death was something called hemochromatosis, a genetic disorder in which the body retains too much iron in the bloodstream. It's a condition that is hard to detect unless you're looking for it, and Becker's father wasn't. Neither was Becker—at least not until 1975, when his doctor noticed hemochromatosis in his family history.

As Becker himself was already forty-five years old, the doctor was concerned: Becker's blood could be a time bomb. The doctor ordered a test that confirmed higher-than-typical amounts of iron in Becker's blood—but, strangely, not as much as one would expect given Becker's age and the fact that he likely had hemochromatosis passed down to him from his father.

The reason may be those Packers tickets. One of the only treatments for hemochromatosis is bloodletting: the removal of some of a patient's blood. As Becker's application for the Packers Fan Hall of Fame explained, by the time he had been diagnosed, he "had sold 145 pints of blood to pay for his season tickets. If he hadn't, he very well may have died like his father." Becker's love of the Packers not only got him into games but quite likely saved his life.

BONUS FACT

The Green Bay Packers name is a reference to the meat packing industry. In 1919, the team's cofounder, Curly Lambeau, secured funding for uniforms from his employer, the Indian Packing Company, on the condition that the team be named for the company. The company itself is long gone, but the name remains—despite protests from the People for the Ethical Treatment of Animals (PETA). In 2000, PETA demanded that the team change their name, suggesting the Pickers (a reference to vegetable picking), or Six-Packers (because of the area's beer industry), but the team refused.

SOVIETS IN DAIRYLAND

When Wisconsin Went (Briefly) Communist

On May 1, 1950, all eyes were on the small town of Mosinee, Wisconsin. At 6 a.m., five armed men raided the house of Ralph Kronenwetter, the mayor of the town (which held about 1,400 residents at this time), leading him to prison. Agents of the self-described United Soviet States of America, they were taking over.

The coup was very well coordinated: The police department was disbanded, and the local newspaper was overtaken as well. The latter even published a picture of Joseph Stalin and an outline of *The Communist Manifesto*, which included calls for no private property, the opening of labor camps, and a ban on religion. Pistol-toting Soviets forced the nuns out of a local Catholic school and ushered them into stockades, and also arrested those who sang hymns in the streets. Executives at the local paper mill—one of the town's biggest employers—were incarcerated. School children were forced to wear uniforms made up of a white shirt and black pants, and the streets were lined with Russian flags. The Communists removed many books from the library, increased grocery prices to prevent a run on supplies, and placed armed patrols in the now-popular soup kitchens in town to maintain order. Even the local restaurant changed cuisine, adding borscht to its menu.

By the next day, however, it was over. No, the American National Guard didn't intervene; they didn't have to. The entire event was a stunt—a mock invasion aimed to reinforce the dangers of communism. The faux coup was the idea of the state's chapter of the American Legion, a national organization of war veterans whose mission includes "foster[ing] patriotism and responsible citizenship." At the time, that mission included ringing the alarm bell about the evils of communism.

Communism was both a real and perceived threat in America; the Soviet Union was the country's main antagonist, with military and weapons rivaling the United States and an appetite for ideological expansion to match. Some Americans—most notably Senator Joseph McCarthy—also used this fear as a cudgel against internal enemies, accusing other Americans of being Communists and, explicitly, un-American. Reacting both to the very real threat of the Soviet Union and the alarmism of McCarthyites, the American Legion believed it was necessary to remind Americans of the nature and risk of a Communist takeover. So, they staged a fake one.

Mosinee itself became the staging ground because of a man named Francis F. Schweinler. He was the owner of the local newspaper, the *Mosinee Times*, a very active member of the state chapter of the American Legion, and a retired brigadier general. Schweinler sent letters to his fellow Mosinee citizens about the ruse, calling it an "object lesson in Americanism" and explaining that the town would be doing a great service to everyone else by "revealing to the world how it is to live under Communists."

The stunt got the attention Schweinler and the American Legion were after. Many papers across the country wrote about the events over the next few days and *Life* magazine, then one of the most influential publications in the country, covered the event in detail. Further, a film crew captured footage of the event for a future documentary. Schweinler and his fellow organizers had told their story in a unique, captivating way.

Unfortunately, the fake takeover wasn't entirely bloodless. Mayor Kronenwetter led a rally at the end of the day, marking the fall of communism in Mosinee. During the rally he suffered a cerebral hemorrhage and lost consciousness, passing away five days later.

BONUS FACT

The American Legion's mission, beyond promoting Americanism, also includes a commitment "to mentoring youth and sponsorship of wholesome programs in our communities" (per its website). Combine patriotism, mentoring, and community programs, and it's no surprise that the Legion holds baseball in high regard (it runs a youth baseball league that dates back to 1925). It was actually as an American Legion Baseball player that future National Baseball Hall of Fame catcher Lawrence Peter Berra became "Yogi Berra." Berra had a habit of sitting with his arms and legs crossed when things went bad in a game, and for this, fellow player Jack Maguire started to call him "Yogi" because he thought Berra looked like a Hindu yogi.

PEACE AND LOVE WIN OUT

The State-Sanctioned Naked Drug-Fest That Saved Lives

The Vietnam War era was among the most controversial in American history. War protestors at the 1968 Democratic National Convention in Chicago clashed with police, leading to hundreds of injuries. And in May 1970, members of the National Guard opened fire on unarmed student protestors, killing four people and wounding nine others at Kent State University.

These violent clashes worried government officials throughout the nation, as they wondered if their communities would be next. For Portland, Oregon, that fear looked like it would become a reality. The American Legion announced President Richard M. Nixon would be addressing their annual convention there that May—just a few weeks after the Kent State incident—to make his case for staying in Vietnam.

Anti-war groups announced their intention to protest. With approximately 25,000 Legionnaires attending the conference and 50,000 protesters likely to arrive, the chance of violence was high. Even though the Legion and the anti-war groups were both guided by principles of nonviolence, it wouldn't take much of a spark to light a true fire between them. An FBI report warned that a clash could be worse than what the nation had just seen in Chicago two years prior. And yet, history books make no mention of a bloody conflict in Portland that spring. Why? Because a bunch of self-professed hippies convinced the governor to throw a party instead.

In the summer of 1969, more than 400,000 people gathered at the Woodstock music festival in Upstate New York. For four days, festival-goers were treated to thirty-two different acts ranging from Grateful Dead to Joan Baez. The concert was an inspiration not only to people at the event but also for those who experienced it vicariously through the retellings of friends and family members. And it gave Oregon an idea.

Anti-war groups, hoping to avoid a clash with police and American Legion members, approached Governor Tom McCall's office with a proposal called "Vortex I: A Biodegradable Festival of Life"—a state-sponsored music festival to be held in the rural areas outside of Portland. It was not-so-coincidentally timed to correspond with the American Legion annual meeting. There were some conditions, though; in order to attract people away from the meeting, the state had to agree to turn a blind eye toward nonviolent crimes and pay for the performances. Activists would have to decide whether to protest at the Legion meeting or enjoy a festival rivaling Woodstock. Surprisingly, McCall agreed to these terms, although he reportedly admitted to an aide that in doing so, he had "committed political suicide."

Between 30,000 and 100,000 people attended Vortex 1, making it one of the largest music festivals of the decade. And the true intention of Vortex 1 was also realized: The American Legion annual meeting was predominantly a peaceful affair (also aided by President Nixon's last-minute cancellation).

McCall pronounced the event a success, telling journalist

Studs Terkel, "it was the damnedest confrontation you'll ever see. We took a park, 20 miles south of Portland, and turned it into an overnight bivouac and disco party. There was a lot of pot smoking and skinny dipping but nobody was killed." The only mistake he made? His prediction as to his own political fortune turned out to be false. He was up for re-election that fall and defeated his Democratic challenger 369,964 to 293,892.

BONUS FACT

Woodstock didn't actually take place at Woodstock, New York; it was in a town called Bethel, New York, about 43 miles away. The festival was really named for the investment group (Woodstock Ventures) which covered the costs of the production. In fact, the festival wasn't originally intended to be in Bethel, either, but in another New York town called Wallkill. Organizers had to relocate the festival to Bethel after Wallkill authorities barred it, arguing that the portable toilets Woodstock was bringing in weren't up to code.

A NEW MEANING TO RECYCLING

The Great Portland Trash Battle of 2002

The Fourth Amendment to the US Constitution protects the "right of the people to be secure in their persons, houses, papers, and effects, against unreasonable searches and seizures," absent a warrant. There are a few exceptions to this, including what happens when you put your garbage out on the curb.

In 1988, the US Supreme Court decided in California v. Greenwood that when you leave something out for the trash collector, you're making it "readily accessible to animals, children, scavengers, snoops, and other members of the public." As a result, the court ruled, you don't have a "reasonable expectation of privacy" over what's in your garbage, and therefore, law enforcement can typically search your trash without impunity. So, that's exactly what police around the country did—and one newspaper really didn't like it.

In March 2002, police in Portland, Oregon, received a tip that one of their own officers had been abusing illegal drugs. The police picked up and sifted through the trash outside the officer's home and found evidence that she was in fact using cocaine, marijuana, and methamphetamine. Given the Greenwood case, this should not have been a problem, but because the officer used a private trash disposal service, the Oregon courts said that the investigating officers overstepped their boundaries. The court ruled that the evidence found in the trash couldn't be used against the officer, and her conviction was overturned.

When the district attorney vowed to appeal, a local newspaper called the *Willamette Week* decided to fight back—by doing some dumpster diving of their own. The newspaper searched the garbage of the district attorney, chief of police, and city's mayor, and then confronted all three with what they found.

The DA was okay with the ruse and jokingly asked the reporters if he had to pay them for removing his garbage that week. But the others didn't appreciate the stunt. The police chief, who at first thought the *Willamette Week* was there to interview him about the practice of rummaging through trash, defended the policy. But when it became clear that they had gone through *his* trash (finding, among other things, something the paper simply described as "a handwritten note scribbled in pencil on a napkin, so personal it made us cringe"), he changed his tune. He stonewalled them as they continued asking questions and, ultimately, issued a press release complaining about the actions of the newspaper.

The mayor's reaction was worse. She summoned the reporters to her office, insisting that they bring the newspapers she had left out in her recycling bin (the only items the reporters had been able to acquire) and that the reporters come with legal counsel. When they arrived, the mayor, saying nothing, simply grabbed back her newspapers and had her press secretary issue the statement: "I consider *Willamette Week*'s actions in this matter to be potentially illegal and absolutely unscrupulous and reprehensible. I will consider all my legal options in response to their actions."

No legal action came, however. The *Willamette Week*, as the

Greenwood case portended, had all the right in the world to go through the garbage. And while they published a comprehensive list of what they found, there was nothing that would have gotten any of their targets into trouble. In fact, the paper concluded, "based on their throwaways, the chief, the DA, and the mayor are squeaky-clean, poop-scooping folks whose private lives are beyond reproach."

BONUS FACT

Portland, Oregon, got its name from the city of Portland, Maine, the hometown of one of the Oregon city's cofounders. The other cofounder was from Boston, Massachusetts, and also wanted to name the new city after his hometown. The solution? The cofounders flipped a coin. The man from Portland won, and the coin used is now on display at the Oregon Historical Society Museum.

A SPY'S DOODY

Why Not All Paper Makes for Good Toilet Paper

Espionage can be dirty work. Actually, as American, French, and British spies learned during the Cold War, it can be *really* dirty work. So dirty, in fact, that step one in their case was simple, straightforward, and a bit disturbing: deprive the Soviets of toilet paper.

At the start of the US/Soviet power struggle, the United States and its allies occupied West Germany, while the Soviet Union occupied East Germany. As *Atlas Obscura* explains, the border was somewhat porous: "Through a reciprocal agreement known as the military liaison missions, the allied nations and the Soviet Union had been permitted to deploy a small number of military intelligence personnel in each other's territory in Germany." The Americans couldn't watch Soviet military exercises, but they soon realized that they *could* obtain Soviet garbage fairly easily.

In general, trash is just that—trash. It lacks any sort of value, especially to someone looking for information. After all, Soviets aren't going to simply throw out a confidential document (or care about what happens to the unimportant things they *do* throw away). The Western powers saw an opportunity, though: If Soviets threw classified documents into the garbage, more information could be recovered. That may seem unlikely, however the American forces realized that the Soviets had made a mistake: The troops assigned to East Germany weren't issued toilet paper. Instead, they were expected to find their own—and unfortunately for them, there wasn't much to be found.

Enter Operation Tamarisk. The allied forces were instructed not to share their toilet paper with their Russian counterparts. By keeping Soviet access to toilet paper scarce, the theory was that the opposing military officials would have to wipe themselves with something else. There typically were not a lot of options, so many had to use an official document that was sitting idly nearby. And because these documents weren't water soluble, they also weren't flushable, so the Russians would use and then toss the classified-document-turned-toilet-paper into a nearby garbage can. The Western spies then came into action, searching through the trash for these papers. What they found there was more than just secret documents (covered in unpleasant "stuff" of course) detailing the covert operations of the Soviet military-industrial complex. The Western counterintelligence agents also found amputated limbs. But when they complained to their superiors, they were ordered to dig even *further*…into the limbs…to investigate the types of shrapnel the Soviets were using.

Luckily, despite the gore and overall grossness of the mission, it was successful. In fact, it is often considered one of the *most* successful intelligence missions of the Cold War.

BONUS FACT

In general, intelligence agencies destroy classified documents as necessary—which is where the term "burn after reading" comes from. The CIA does exactly that and in a way that conserves energy. According to TalkingPointsMemo.com, the exhaust from the incinerator used to burn documents is used to heat water at CIA headquarters.

SOLD OUT BY...POOP?

Why You May Not Want to Relieve Yourself at Joseph Stalin's House

When two world leaders meet—in front of the cameras at least—it's all smiles and handshakes. Behind the scenes, however, the intelligence agencies of each nation are constantly trying to learn as much as possible about the other nation, covertly or otherwise. And when it comes to getting that information advantage, there are few boundaries; spies will do whatever it takes to find out what the other party is thinking.

The same was true during the heyday of communism—even among Communist leaders. During the 1940s and 1950s, Soviet leader Joseph Stalin and Chinese chairman Mao Zedong had a solid relationship, but trust can only go so far. While both were leaders of Communist nations during the height of the Cold War, they were cautious about one another—to a degree, they were even competing against each other to become the de facto leader of the broader Communist movement. The two met face-to-face a number of times during the era, including in the winter of 1949, when Mao made a state visit to Russia.

Stalin wanted to learn more about his Chinese counterpart—and not just by talking to Mao. Despite their positive relationship, Stalin apparently decided that a bit of spying was in order. So according to former Soviet operative Igor Atamanenko, he made an investment in some new plumbing.

Spy methods were less sophisticated back then—technology didn't allow for tiny cameras or listening devices. But one thing that the advancements of those days *could* do was analyze stool. Doctors often (and still do) used stool samples to help detect diseases and other health concerns; Stalin wondered if the same technique could be used to build a more in-depth personal profile of his intelligence targets. As Atamanenko told the BBC, "If [Soviet scientists] detected high levels of amino acid Tryptophan, they concluded that person was calm and approachable," but "a lack of potassium in poo was seen as a sign of a nervous disposition and someone with insomnia."

Whether those conclusions are scientifically proven is another matter: It was good enough for Stalin. According to *The Telegraph*, "special lavatories were installed for Mao's ten-day visit in order for the Chinese leader's stool to be collected in secret boxes instead of the sewers." At least, that's the former spy's story; the modern Russian government neither confirms nor denies these events.

BONUS FACT

Not everyone thinks about toilets as much as Joseph Stalin did. Certainly NASA didn't…at least not when Alan Shepard was set to become the first American in space. The flight only took fifteen minutes and twenty-two seconds from launch to splashdown (a spacecraft landing method that uses a parachute), so NASA didn't think Shepard would need to use the facilities. They were wrong. Because of various delays, Shepard spent more than five hours in his spacesuit, which didn't come with a way for him to relieve himself safely. Before launch, he radioed in, saying, "Man, I gotta pee." NASA, not wanting to delay the mission further, allowed him to do so in his suit.

THE REPLACEMENTS
The Soviet Union's Secret Hockey Team

Joseph Stalin ruled the Soviet Union for more than three decades, using the threat of violence as a significant tool in keeping enemies at bay. The death toll from his regime is difficult to estimate, however, and Stalin's government didn't keep track of its crimes (how convenient). But most agree that the number of lives taken during his reign is north of ten million depending on whether you count the victims of famines. Regardless, it's safe to say that most Soviets—even those close to Stalin—rightfully feared him. Including a man named Vasily Dzhugashvili. Even though he was Stalin's own son.

Dzhugashvili was born in 1921, just one year before his father became the singular leader of the Soviet Union. Dzhugashvili's mother, Nadezhda Alliluyeva, was Stalin's second wife; the two married in 1919 when Alliluyeva was between seventeen and eighteen years old and Stalin was a forty-one-year-old widower with a twelve-year-old son. The marriage between Dzhugashvili's parents was relatively short-lived—and not because of the age difference. In 1932, Alliluyeva died under suspicious circumstances.

The official cause of death was appendicitis, but this doesn't explain why her body was found holding a gun. The timing of her death was also odd: She and Stalin had just had a public argument at a dinner party. Dzhugashvili was only eleven at the time of his mother's death. His younger sister, Svetlana, was only six.

Stalin didn't step in as the primary caretaker of his two children from Alliluyeva. Instead, he had guards and servants act as their guardians. But despite losing his mother and rarely seeing his father, Vasily found success in the Red Air Force. He rose in rank faster than most others in the force, becoming Commander of the Air Forces of the Moscow Military District before his thirtieth birthday. And by the late 1940s, he was also the president of VVS Moscow, the air force's sports club. Dzhugashvili was therefore in charge of a very public element of Soviet national pride.

But on January 5, 1950, a tragedy put all of this success at risk. That day, most of the Soviet hockey team (eleven of the thirteen players, plus the team doctor and a masseur) were involved in a plane crash on the way to a match. The plane had tried to land despite extreme weather conditions—a snowstorm with strong wind. All nineteen people on board, including the six-person crew, died.

In most cases, a tragedy like this would have resulted in a national day of mourning and a state funeral. But in this case, the exact opposite happened: Dzhugashvili hid the crash from his father and all of the Soviet Union. It's believed that Dzhugashvili may have been to blame for the tragedy, especially given future events in his career. In 1952, he would be dismissed from the air force for another tragedy in which he allowed planes to fly despite bad weather. Regardless, Dzhugashvili feared his father's wrath. So he decided to cover up the accident, pretending it never happened. This plan required a team, however, so the next day, Dzhugashvili made sure he had one in place. As *The New York*

Times reported, he "immediately recruited a new team, and his father apparently never knew the difference."

Perhaps Stalin just wasn't much of a hockey fan—or perhaps the replacements were good enough players to complete Dzhugashvili's ruse. And their record is certainly evidence to that end. In 1951, a national annual hockey tournament called the Soviet Cup debuted in the USSR, and VVS Moscow came in second place. The next year, VVS Moscow won the cup.

BONUS FACT

After his father's death in 1953, Dzhugashvili spent most of his remaining years in prison as an enemy of the state, eventually dying in 1962—just a few days shy of his forty-first birthday. But his younger sister, Svetlana (who used her mother's last name, Alliluyeva), met a different fate: escape. In 1967, she defected to the United States.

H&R BLOCKED SHOTS

The NHL's Perfect Goalie—
Who Can Also Do Your Taxes

The words "emergency" and "accountant" aren't usually seen near each other, and if they are, it's rarely for a fun reason. But if you do need an accountant in such a situation, you want this person to be perfect; metaphorically speaking, you want someone who will make sure nothing gets by her or him. When you're a hockey team, the metaphor becomes literal—as a certified public accountant named Scott Foster learned on the evening of March 29, 2018. On this night, Foster wasn't there to do the team's taxes. He was there to protect their net.

Hockey players often get hurt, and goalies are no exception. In general, NHL teams only carry two goalies on their twenty-three-man roster. That's almost always sufficient: If the first-string goalie is injured during the game, you have a backup. And if he is injured between games, a team can typically promote a player from their minor league franchise and use the other goalie (previously used as a backup player) as the starter until the first-stringer is ready to return. Having both goalies fall to injury in the same game is extraordinarily rare, though it can happen, and the National Hockey

League has a rule to account for this: The home team is required to have two emergency goalies at the ready who can suit up for either team if needed. As the pro players are already either in uniform at the game or honing their skills at a minor league rink, teams usually fulfill this requirement by finding amateurs—men who still suit up for a local recreational team but haven't played competitively since college. The amateur goalie comes to the game as a spectator—he doesn't suit up or hang out with the team but gets the VIP treatment otherwise; the AP describes this experience as "a nice dinner and a night in the press box watching the world's best players compete at hockey's highest level."

Scott Foster was one of these amateur goalies—one of a handful in the Chicago Blackhawks' rotation—and coming into that March evening, he had never entered a game. During pregame warm-ups, the Blackhawks' intended starting goalie, Anton Forsberg, got hurt. The backup was a man named Collin Delia, who had just been called up from the minor leagues earlier that day. When Foster himself arrived at the arena, he was ushered to the locker room, not the press box. He signed an amateur contract (unpaid) and the equipment manager quickly made him a jersey with his last name and the number 90 on the back. He sat in the team's locker room to watch the game, and the expectation was that he would remain there for the entire game.

However, things didn't go according to plan. Delia would later tell ESPN that he was "getting absolutely bombarded" in the second period of the match and began cramping. The team's trainers gave him IV fluids in hopes that he could play out the third and final period, but, with fourteen minutes and one second left, his body gave out and Foster was sent in to protect the Blackhawks' four-goal lead.

Amazingly, the accountant in hockey pads succeeded. For the remainder of the game, the visiting Winnipeg Jets assailed the amateur with shot after shot—seven in total. He stopped all seven, and the Blackhawks won, 6-2. As Foster exited the ice, the crowd (approximately 21,000 fans) chanted his name.

BONUS FACT

Traditionally, NHL goalies always wore the number one as their uniform number, but over the years, deviations from this tradition have become increasingly common. However, there are two numbers you won't see *any* NHL goalie wearing anytime soon: zero and double-zero. According to ESPN, this is due to a software limitation: "The NHL doesn't allow the single or double doughnut because they cannot be registered in the league's database."

FRANKLIN'S INTEREST

What Happens When You Mix Money, Multiplication, and Not Much Else

Compound interest—which Albert Einstein is said to have called "the most powerful force in the universe"—is the simple idea that when initial money (known as the "principal") deposited into a bank collects interest and that interest is added to the principal, the interest itself begins collecting interest. The money builds upon itself, allowing the person holding the bank account to build up a sizable war chest over time.

But what if you kept the money in your account, earning interest for decades or even *centuries*? How would accountants handle that? To answer this, all you need do is look to Ben Franklin, who made exactly that type of investment.

In his will, Franklin left 1,000 pounds each—equivalent to approximately $4,400 in US currency—to the cities of Philadelphia and Boston. But the cities were not given access to the money immediately. Instead, Franklin required that the money be held in trust for one hundred years after his death (which was in 1790). After that, the cities could remove a portion of the trust money to establish a trade school. But the remaining money had to remain in the bank for another one hundred years.

Franklin's investment paid out handsomely. When he placed the money in the trusts in 1785, the 2,000 pounds combined would have been worth about $100,000 to $125,000 US dollars in 2013. When the trusts became due in 1990, Philadelphia's was worth $2 million. Boston's trust, from which less money had been withdrawn following the first century, was worth $5 million. Philadelphia used the $2 million to provide scholarships for local high schoolers. Boston used the $5 million to fund the Benjamin Franklin Institute of Technology, which was established out of the smaller portion of the trust withdrawn one hundred years earlier.

You may wonder what would happen if Franklin had required that the trust remain for *another* century. In that case, the trust may be ruled illegal. As recounted by *Lapham's Quarterly*, in 1938, a lawyer named Jonathan Holdeen divided $2.5 million into a series of trusts, each of which had 500- or 1,000-year locks on them. One of the trusts was given to the Unitarian Church, another to Hartwick College in New York, and another to the state of Pennsylvania, as a way to honor Ben Franklin for inspiring the idea. Holdeen's goal was to make it so that the citizens of the state never had to pay taxes again—starting in the year 2938 or so.

These trusts, known as the Holdeen Trusts, soon ran into a problem. The size of an ever-growing trust of that starting size and duration could outpace the net worth of the known universe. Holdeen himself estimated that the trust for the Unitarian Church itself could reach $2.5 quadrillion (that's 2.5 million billions) by the time it became payable.

Litigation hit full swing after Holdeen's death in 1967, and in 1977, a judge ruled that the trusts could remain for however many centuries Holdeen required, but the interest had to be paid out to the beneficiary each year. Hartwick College, therefore, gets about $450,000 annually from their Holdeen Trust and, in or around 2936, will receive a lump sum payment of $9 million.

BONUS FACT

Lawyers often hold money "in escrow" on behalf of their clients. For example, when someone purchases a house, the down payment gets put into escrow until the closing occurs (typically sixty to ninety days later). As these small amounts of money are in the bank for a small amount of time, the administrative costs of dealing with the interest negates the value. In 1983, New York implemented a solution by setting up an IOLA Fund. IOLA ("Interest on Lawyer Accounts") acts as a pooled bank account, allowing the administrative costs to be managed centrally. The interest is used to help defray legal costs for poor, elderly, and disabled residents.

NO COPYING THE QUEEN

The Strange Legal Warning on British Money

If you happen to have a £5 note on you, take it out for a moment. (If not, you can easily find pictures on the Bank of England's website.) Since September 2016, £5 notes have featured Queen Elizabeth II on one side and Winston Churchill on the other. And below Churchill, in the bottom left corner, you'll see a copyright notice. Specifically, it reads: "© The Governor and Company of the Bank of England," followed by the print year.

This may seem extraordinarily unnecessary—if you make near-perfect replicas of real notes, it's called counterfeiting, and it's illegal. So why does British currency also need a copyright warning?

Well, people were accepting bills that were obviously fake in lieu of real currency. Why? Because it was art.

In 1984, an artist now known as J.S.G. Boggs was in a diner in Chicago enjoying a cup of coffee with a doughnut. He began to doodle on a napkin. As *The New York Times* explained, "he started with the numeral 1, then transformed it into the image of a dollar bill." This caught the eye of his waitress who wanted to buy it off him, but he declined. Instead, the two came up with a seemingly silly idea: She'd accept it as payment for his ninety-cent meal. She even gave him ten cents back as change.

For the rest of his life, Boggs tried to repeat this type of exchange. Instead of actual money, he'd offer up a hand-drawn, high-quality image of one side of a piece of currency. And every so often, he'd find someone who said yes. The denominations and even the issuing nations would change—he'd draw the right amount of money to cover the tab and use currency appropriate for where he was. He'd sign each note, sometimes making himself the Secretary of the Treasury. Over time, these little works became known as "Boggs notes" in the art world, and collectors would buy them for well above their face value. Boggs never sold them directly to dealers, though, instead continuing to use them in commerce. He'd then sell the receipt and change—and the info as to where he used the Boggs note—to collectors and galleries. At some point in the late 1990s, a collector bought just one Boggs bill for $420,000. By 1999, *The Economist* reported, "his drawings had paid for more than $1m-worth of goods, including rent, clothes, hotels and a brand-new Yamaha motorbike." His fake money was a win-win for everyone involved!

But not everyone was pleased with his efforts. At a certain point, even a hand-drawn, one-sided bill is a counterfeit, right? That's what the United Kingdom believed, at least. In 1986, as he set up for a gallery showing in London, Boggs was arrested. As the *Times* recounts, "three constables raided the gallery and hauled Mr. Boggs off to jail. He was charged with four counts of violating the Forgery and Counterfeiting Act." He hired a civil rights lawyer named Geoffrey Robertson who argued that no, this wasn't illegal. Again, they were hand-drawn, one-sided, and now obviously art—and the UK courts agreed.

The government gave up on charging Boggs, but not before it protected itself from similar problems in the future.

If counterfeiting wasn't a viable legal "gotcha," there was another one: copyright. As Robertson would later explain, the UK added the copyright notice to their notes in response to Boggs's victory in the counterfeiting case.

BONUS FACT

Not all British currency is vegan-friendly. In 2016, the Bank of England issued a new £5 note made of a polymer (instead of paper), as it lasts longer and allows for better security features. Not everyone was happy about the change, however; it turned out that the polymer currency used small amounts of animal fat in the production process. Despite petitions to change the formula, though, the bank announced in the summer 2017 that tallow-containing banknotes were here to stay.

THE YOLK'S ON YOU

Why Funny-Looking Eggs Are
No Laughing Matter

Many people find clowns to be creepy or downright scary, so apologies for this next visual: Close your eyes for a moment and imagine the face of a circus clown. You'll probably settle on a powder-white face with an exaggerated red nose, but beyond that, the details will vary. Maybe your imaginary clown has droopy blue eyes and a frown. Perhaps he has a huge mop of rainbow hair or tiny purple dimples drawn on his cheeks. Maybe he is a she, with blond locks and a cowboy hat.

To the nonclown public, these unique details aren't terribly important. But to the clowns themselves, they are. Take that sad clown, for example. The person behind the makeup is, for all intents and purposes, an actor—one who has probably spent years crafting his character. Beyond the face makeup, he has to embody the role of someone who is inconsolably upset (except for a glimmer of happiness here or there right before he gets a deluge of seltzer shot into his face). The details of his makeup help define that character, and it's likely that he's spent more time than you'd think in refining every brushstroke. Much like a painter wouldn't take kindly to someone else copying his work, this sad clown would probably be *truly* upset if another clown happened to don the same face. So how does a clown prevent this from happening?

The answer: eggs. Yes, the twelve-to-a-carton ones that come from chickens.

The explanation for this starts with copyright law. In the United States, you can only get copyright over a creation if the work is "fixed in any tangible medium of expression." The definition isn't an exact science, but there are some examples which aren't debated—the words in a book or a painting on a canvas for instance. The word "fixed" means that the work has to be put into a permanent form. Fake noses, face makeup, and wigs don't work, because sooner or later, you're going to take them off.

So if painting your face doesn't earn you copyright protection over your design, what about painting it on something else? Something oval, like your head—and if it's already eggshell white, like your makeup, even better! Sounds a lot like an egg, right? And that's essentially what the Clown Egg Register is.

In 1946, a Londoner named Stan Bult—whom the BBC describes as "a chemist by trade, though not a clown himself"—decided to capture the faces of the clowns who entertained him on the shells of eggs in hopes of ensuring that wannabes didn't copy their looks. By the time of his death twenty years later, Bult had created a library of two hundred such eggs—a de facto library of clowns who performed in and around the UK's capital city. And the city's clowns used that library as a way to ensure that they weren't encroaching on another's designs.

After Bult's death, Clowns International (yes, there's an international brotherhood of clowns) took over the efforts. Today, there are dozens of eggs in the register, each atop a pedestal and painted and dressed to mimic the design of a professional clown. The eggs can be seen on display at the Clowns Gallery-Museum in the village of Wookey Hole in Somerset, England. In 2018, photographer Luke Stephenson and his cohort, a clown named Helen Champion, also put together a book featuring photos of 169 of the portraits.

BONUS FACT

Bozo the Clown is probably America's most famous clown, but you may be surprised to discover that he's not one person. Over Bozo's history, multiple performers have donned the red nose and terrifying makeup. In fact, Bozo has been franchised, allowing him to appear in multiple markets at the same time.

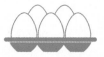

THE GREAT ATLANTIC EGG DEBATE

Why You Can't Buy British Eggs in America,
and Vice Versa

Salmonella is a type of bacteria that can make you dangerously sick. It's most commonly found in uncooked chicken, meat, and eggs, and while you can avoid it if you prepare and cook your food properly, accidents happen. For example, you might eat some uncooked cake batter that has raw egg in it. For this reason, it's crucial that steps be taken to keep salmonella away from your eggs as much as possible. That's why, in the United States, grocers refrigerate their eggs. It's also why, in the United Kingdom, grocers *don't* refrigerate their eggs. Yes, that's right: The US and the UK can't agree on the safest way to store chicken eggs.

When a chicken lays an egg, the egg is exposed to whatever else is under the chicken. This often includes chicken droppings, and those droppings can contain salmonella. Eggshells are somewhat porous, so any salmonella-laden chicken poop can contaminate the egg. However, nature provides a solution: Freshly laid eggs also come with a thin external membrane called a cuticle which envelops the shell, providing an additional barrier between the inside of the egg and the outside world.

The cuticle isn't foolproof, of course, and many feel that if the dirt on the outside of the egg can make you sick, it shouldn't be entering the chain of commerce. As a result, United States law requires that commercial egg farms wash their eggs before putting them up for sale. However, if cold water is used (and it usually is), the yolk and whites inside the shell contract, leaving more room for bacteria to enter. And if the egg isn't fully dried after it is washed, moisture can take hold, giving bacteria yet another chance to multiply. This isn't the only way salmonella can get inside the egg: It can also be transmitted directly from the chicken. That is, if a live chicken is carrying salmonella, any eggs laid by that chicken also run the risk of carrying the bacteria. If those eggs are then stored at room temperature, the salmonella bacteria will thrive. For these reasons, the US mandates that its eggs always be refrigerated.

But there's an alternative: the UK way. Here—and, for that matter, most of the world—the policy is to leave the egg unwashed before sale, keeping the cuticle intact. However, refrigeration of the unwashed eggs is generally a bad idea; to minimize bacterial growth, you don't want to move eggs from warm to cold and back again. So, the UK requires that eggs be sold unrefrigerated. And to account for those egg-laying chickens already stricken with salmonella, the UK uses the money they save in refrigeration costs to vaccinate their chickens.

Wash, don't wash; refrigerate, don't refrigerate: There is no finite answer. As chef and food writer J. Kenji López-Alt noted, "In the US, eggs are cleaner to begin with but more prone to re-contamination. Elsewhere, the interiors are safer from contamination but the shells themselves could have baddies in them. It's a trade-off either way." Regardless, the best way for consumers to stay safe is the same wherever you are: Wash your eggs before use, and always fully cook them before consumption.

BONUS FACT

Do you wash raw chicken before cooking it? You probably shouldn't—and this is something both the UK *and* the US agree on. The US Food and Drug Administration's website notes that rinsing the birds "makes it more likely for bacteria to spread to areas around the sink and countertops." The UK's National Health Service has a similar warning on its website, saying "splashing water from washing chicken under a tap can spread the bacteria onto hands, work surfaces, clothing, and cooking equipment."

LOVE MEANS NOTHING IN TENNIS

The History of the Sport's Unique Scoring System

Love-15-30-40. If you've ever played tennis, or just enjoy watching it, you know that this is the game's basic scoring system. And you probably think it makes no sense whatsoever. If you're counting by 15, you hit 45, not 40. And "love" isn't a number at all!

It's a weird system. And there's a good amount of debate as to why this is the scoring, with the most likely explanation involving a weird confluence of eggs, the English, clocks, and the inability to divide an odd number by two without a resulting remainder.

Let's start with the eggs. Eggs are, of course, oval-shaped, much like the number zero. And in a few sports, they're used as such: "Goose egg" is a common phrase in American sports, and "duck," short for "duck's egg," is common in cricket. It is believed that tennis is also included in this list. Why? Tennis originated in France in the twelfth century, and many of the rules and terminology created at this time for the sport have been carried through history and across countries. One of these terms is the French word for "the egg": "*l'oeuf*." If you're not a French speaker, this term sounds a lot like the English word "love." It is likely that a series of English speakers simply replaced the French word with its English homophone.

As for the numbers 15, 30, and eventually 40? The most likely explanation involves a pretty simple way to keep score: clock faces. The first point in a game would earn you one quarter of a revolution around your clock, or 15 (minutes or seconds). The second point moved you to 30, and the third to 45. When the game ended, both opponents' clocks would be reset. Easy—except that tennis games have to be won by two or more points. If both players were on a 45, then what? Moving the hand halfway to 60 wouldn't work: There's no 52.5 on a clock.

A little creativity was in order. The solution: Move the hand to 40 for the third point, instead of 45. When players tied at 40-40 ("deuce"), the next point would be worth 10, moving the clock to 50. If the same player earned the subsequent point, he or she would get another ten points and win the game. If not, his or her clock would be reset to 40, and the players would be tied at deuce again until one player scored two consecutive points.

There are alternative theories given for both oddities as well. Given how far back the origins of the sport date, the full story behind the scoring lies only with those who are since long gone. However, given what *is* known, the previously detailed theories are most likely.

BONUS FACT

In the heat of the moment, a tennis player may end up shouting out a curse word or two. But in many tournaments, that's against the rules. If a player swears and the chair umpire hears it, the umpire may cite the player for a code violation (multiple violations can lead to the loss of points, games, or even the entire match). This means umpires need to know what words are curse words. As some tournaments feature players from all around the world—Wimbledon, for example—organizers provide umpires with a list of banned words from many different languages. The umpires are then expected to memorize that list.

A LITTLE COLOR GOES A LONG WAY

Why Tennis Balls Are Yellow

In the spring of 2018, a debate raged on *Twitter* about a question that you might think easy to answer: What color is a tennis ball? Yet, it proved to be a bit harder for people to agree on. Some said yellow, others said green. Even champion tennis player Roger Federer chimed in ("It's yellow, right?"). Fortunately, there is an answer to this question; Federer was right—they are in fact yellow. If you really want to insist that they are green for the sake of avoiding that "I told you so" from a friend, that's fine, too; there is a bigger question here, after all: Why aren't tennis balls white? Or, more accurately, why aren't they white *anymore*?

That's right: tennis balls used to be white—and as recently as the mid-1980s! When top pros took to England to participate in the annual Wimbledon tournament of 1986, for example, they weren't hitting yellow balls, but white ones. So, what changed? TV.

TVs first became commercially viable in the 1920s, and then became commonplace in consumer homes over the next decade. In 1937, the BBC aired a tennis match at Wimbledon for the first time. But it didn't look like the matches you see on your TV nowadays. For the first thirty years of Wimbledon on TV, it was broadcast in black-and-white, as for most of that time period, the color TV hadn't been invented. The white tennis balls were easy to see in this two-color format.

Then in the 1960s, color TVs became increasingly popular, and the sports world had to react. In 1967, the BBC broadcast the Wimbledon tournament in color for the first time. You might think this would be a wonderful change, but the experience wasn't great for fans watching at home. The reason? The white tennis balls. As *Tennis Week* noted, "research showed that TV viewers had a tougher time seeing the ball in motion on the courts." Further, as an ESPN TV producer reported, the balls "turned green from grass stains. They blended so much with the grass the visuals were compromised."

In the 1970s, the International Tennis Federation responded by looking for a nonwhite option for tournament balls. After much research, they decided on a color that would appear well on TV: fluorescent yellow. Though this color may not be appealing to many, it made it a lot easier for tennis fans watching matches at home. In 1972, the ITF officially authorized the yellow tennis balls for competitive use.

In 1986, Wimbledon—the final holdout of tennis's four major tournaments—finally gave in to the needs of advancing technology and adopted the yellow ball. Since then, players of all levels and abilities have done the same, even though few will ever play a match on TV. And today, most take for granted that tennis balls are yellow (or lime green, if you prefer to call it that color).

BONUS FACT

No matter what the color, tennis balls have to bounce. But they can't bounce too much or too little, or else they won't meet regulations. Want to test your own tennis balls? Unlike most experiments, there's one you actually can try at home! According to the ITF, the test involves "dropping the ball vertically from a height of 254 cm (100 inches) and measuring the rebound, which should be 135–147 cm (53–58 inches)."

COLOR YOUR FEELINGS

Giving New Meaning to the Phrase
"Feeling Blue"

When you take a pill, it makes its way to your stomach where it eventually dissolves. The materials that the pill is made of (or for capsules, what is inside the pill) make their way into your bloodstream. Some of these ingredients cause chemical reactions that block pain, reduce swelling, open blood vessels, or go to war against infections. Regardless of the pill's intended purpose, taking it doesn't take much, if any, thought. It does all the work.

Or perhaps it doesn't. Before you put the pill into your mouth, you look at what you're taking. And, perhaps subconsciously, you notice something about the pill that you might think doesn't matter: what color it is. The color of the pill shouldn't affect how well the pill works, of course—but surprisingly, it may.

Studies have shown that while you shouldn't judge a pill by its cover (just as you shouldn't judge a book similarly), you can't help yourself. And this judgment leads to a classic example of the placebo effect. You already associate certain colors with certain moods, situational outcomes, etc., and those associations don't disappear when the colored item is your medication. As a result, certain colors of pills thrive at reaching different medical goals. *The Atlantic* shares the basics of this color code: "Blue pills act best as sedatives. Red and orange are stimulants. Cheery yellows make the most effective antidepressants, while green reduces anxiety and white soothes pain. Brighter colors and embossed brand names further strengthen these effects—a bright yellow pill with the name on its surface, for example, may have a stronger effect than a dull yellow pill without it."

However, as *The Atlantic* further explains, that color system isn't universal—cultural differences can have an impact. For instance, the sedative power of blue doesn't work on Italian men. The scientists who discovered this anomaly think it's due to "gli Azzuri" (the Blues), Italy's national soccer team. Because they associate the color blue with the drama of a match, it actually gets their adrenaline pumping. And yellow's connotations change in Africa, where it's associated with better antimalarial drugs, as eye whites can turn yellowish when a person is suffering from the disease.

The good news is that drug manufacturers are quite aware of this quirk of your consciousness and act accordingly. That's why you don't often see black pills, which most people associate with darkness, despair, and death. It's not foolproof, of course; there's no way to account for how you as an individual associate colors with the world around you. But the other solution would be to take your pills without looking at them first—and that would be a very bad idea.

BONUS FACT

Pills can be used for more than treating medical conditions: They can also read your email! Well, at least a prototype pill could. In 2013, Motorola developed an "authentication vitamin"—a pill which could turn your body into a password emitter. Roberta Dugan, the project lead, explained the tech to *AllThingsD*: "When you swallow it, the acids in your stomach serve as the electrolyte, and they power it up and the switch goes on and off and it creates an 18-bit ECG-like signal in your body. Essentially, your entire body becomes your authentication token." Basically, the pill is a swallowable, digestible microcomputer that—so long as it's still in your belly—allows you to log into your devices with nothing more than a touch. The pill has gained FDA approval but is still a ways off from being available to the noncyborg public.

SON OF A BRICK!

Why Stepping On a LEGO Hurts So Much

LEGO "bricks," as the individual pieces in a LEGO set are called, are great toys, unlocking the creativity and manual dexterity of children (and adults!) around the world. You can do almost anything with them: Build iconic scenes from sci-fi movies, construct vehicles that defy physics—even piece together something purely from your imagination. But there's one thing you should absolutely, positively, never do with a LEGO brick: Step on it with bare feet. Why not? Well, it hurts—a lot.

But you probably knew that already; after all, who *hasn't* stepped on one of the tiny 16-by-24-by-9.6 mm bricks and screamed in agony? For a little toy, LEGO bricks can bring a world of pain. Here's why: First, LEGO bricks are exceptionally sturdy—they have to be, otherwise, they wouldn't be such great building materials. Step on fallen cereal pieces and they'll shatter under your weight into a pile of dust. Stomp on an egg and you'll have a mess on your hands (well, your kitchen floor at least). But step on a LEGO brick and it'll survive just fine. According to a BBC report, a single LEGO brick can resist 950 pounds of mass pressing down on it. Put into LEGO terms, you can stack approximately 375,000 LEGO bricks on top of one another before the bottom one will crack. They're tough.

Your feet, on the other hand, are sensitive—more so than most of your other body parts. There are as many as 200,000 nerve endings on the soles of each of your feet—that's why they are ticklish, why reflexology is a thing, and why it's generally a very good idea to wear shoes. It's also a large part of why LEGO bricks can wreak havoc.

But that's only part of the equation. The shape of the LEGO brick—specifically the raised dots and sharp corners—matters as well. New York University physics professor Tycho Sleator told *Quartz* that "When you step on something with a sharp corner, the force from the corner is concentrated over a very small region of your foot. This would result in a very high pressure on that small region of your foot." And that, of course, means pain.

And finally, there are the children. Because grownups exert more force when they walk than kids do (simply because adults are larger—they are called "grown-ups" for a reason!), stepping on a LEGO brick hurts them more than it does children. An eight-year-old can step on a LEGO brick with near-impunity, so there's less incentive for them to do a thorough cleanup after playing (okay, so that doesn't actually increase the amount of pain *you* feel, but it does make it more likely that you'll start wearing hard-soled slippers around the house).

BONUS FACT

In the early 1980s, LEGO gave some of their longest-standing employees a token of appreciation. If you worked there for twenty-five years, you were given a solid, 14-carat gold LEGO brick. You can't buy one in stores, but one made it to *eBay* in 2012, selling for approximately $12,500.

TAKE TWO OF THESE AND CALL THE SNAKE MORTICIAN IN THE MORNING

Why Fighting Snakes Can Be Quite the Pill

If you live in the US, it's called acetaminophen. In the UK, it's called paracetamol. But most likely, you know it as Tylenol's active ingredient. For humans, it's a rather useful drug, aiding with headaches, fever, and more. Of course, there are some people who shouldn't take Tylenol, and you most certainly can overdose on it if you take too much. However, by and large, it's helpful, and safe enough to buy without a prescription.

If you're living in Guam, acetaminophen can also be the solution to a very specific, island-wide headache: the brown tree snake. Brown tree snakes and Tylenol do *not* mix well. The fatal dose of acetaminophen for this species is as little as 80 mg, or about the amount you'd find in a quarter of one regular-strength Tylenol pill.

The brown tree snake isn't native to Guam, but it certainly made a home for itself there. As of 2013, there were two million brown tree snakes on the tiny Pacific island. It is not known how exactly the first snakes arrived on Guam; the best guess is that they accidentally came over on a cargo plane as stowaways. As the snakes don't have many natural predators on the island, it was hard to control their population. They also create a massive amount of damage. They eat the birds native to the island and have wiped out as many as ten different bird species. In turn, the lowered bird population has reduced the number of new saplings in Guam's forests, as there aren't enough birds to spread the seeds from existing trees. And fewer trees meant a reduced habitat for other animals.

Enter acetaminophen. The US government realized that feeding little bits of the drug to these snakes would wipe out a lot of the population of snakes in this US territory—they just needed to find a way to deliver the medication. This is not as easy as it may sound, though. First, there were a lot of snakes, and it would take a huge amount of time and resources to administer doses of Tylenol by hand. In another unhelpful twist, it was very hard to travel through the jungles to *find* the snakes to dose because of a huge number of spiders and spiderwebs everywhere. (Why so many spiders? Because there weren't enough birds left to keep their populations in check.) Blanketing the area with acetaminophen wouldn't work either, as it would put the lives of other animals at risk (including those they wanted to protect from the snakes). So the anti-snake brigade had to get a little bit creative.

That's when mice entered the picture—and not just any mice: mice paratroopers! In December 2013, the US military outfitted two thousand dead mice with cardboard-and-tissue-paper parachutes, filled them with micro-doses of acetaminophen, and loaded them into helicopters. The helicopters then flew the mice "bombs" on a low-altitude flight, as NBC News reported, "dropping their furry bundles on a timed sequence" so that they would hang on the forest canopy. There—out of the reach of most other animals—they waited as a tempting but fatal snack for the brown tree snakes.

The experiment, which cost about $8 million, was mostly successful—but it was only a small test. Unfortunately, two thousand mice aren't enough to make a meaningful dent in a population of two million snakes (and dropping millions of dead mice isn't realistic for *anyone's* budget or schedule). As a result, Guam remains a brown tree snake haven—and looks as though it will be for the foreseeable future.

BONUS FACT

Overdosing on Tylenol can be fatal and isn't as uncommon as you'd think. An easy solution: replacing bottles, which allow a person to pour out as many pills as he or she wants, with blister packs, which require more effort to remove a smaller amount of medication. In 1998, Britain mandated that paracetamol pills sold over the counter in amounts greater than sixteen, or at the pharmacy in amounts greater than thirty-two, had to be sold in blister packs. As *The New York Times* reported: "A study by Oxford University researchers showed that over the subsequent eleven or so years, suicide deaths from Tylenol overdoses declined by 43 percent."

BEHOLD THE PARATROOPING RODENT

*Why It May Be Okay to Drop
Beavers from Airplanes*

The Humane Society of the United States—an organization dedicated to animal protection—has a webpage titled "What to Do About Beavers." The problem these animals cause is a pretty simple one: They build dams, which is a very good thing if they're in a relatively rural floodplain, but a really bad thing if they are in more densely populated suburbs or cities. Left unchecked, beavers in an area with a lot of humans can cause major damage to trees and, in some cases, flooding.

The Humane Society, therefore, understands that it's necessary to take action against the beaver population at times. The organization suggests against trapping or shooting the animals, which (beyond being inhumane) is ineffective. As they explain, "it only creates a vacuum into which new beavers will move, often sooner rather than later." Instead, they offered a few suggestions, such as fencing off trees and painting the trees with an abrasive coating. They do not, however, suggest parachuting urban beavers into rural areas—but they probably should.

(Do not try this at home.)

In 1948, Idaho had a beaver problem. As people moved into old beaver habitats and started building houses, the animals became an increasingly sinister menace. The Idaho Fish and Game department thus wanted to relocate the beavers to the uninhabited parts of the state. A man named Elmo W. Heter first tried to collect the beavers and put them on mules for transport, but this wasn't successful. As he'd later recount in a paper on his efforts, the mules "become spooky and quarrelsome when loaded with a struggling, odorous pair of live beavers." Undeterred, Heter tried a new approach: He took an older male beaver who would soon be dubbed Geronimo and dropped it from an airplane.

Heter's process went like this: First, using weights, the Idaho Fish and Game department tested crates until they found a type that would stay closed until reaching the ground. Then, Geronimo's job began. Heter dropped him multiple times from a plane and onto the field below in order to determine the appropriate drop height and further test the crates. Once Geronimo had safely landed enough times for Heter's liking, the beaver relocation went into full swing.

The relocation, by and large, was a success. In the fall of 1948, seventy-six live beavers were dropped, with only one casualty. In this case, a rope broke, opening the box as it was released.

As unfortunate as this instance was, observations made late in 1949 showed all of the remaining airborne transplanting to be successful. The beavers had built dams, constructed houses, stored up food, and were well on their way to producing colonies in these rural areas.

Heter estimated that transporting four beavers in this fashion could be accomplished at the relatively low price of $30 (about $300 in 2018) and concluded that "the savings in man-hours, and in the mortality of animals, is quite evident," in case anyone wanted to repeat the process. And, according to the *Smithsonian* magazine, the air-dropped beavers' descendants still populate the region today! But don't expect any more beavers to be tossed out of airplanes any time soon: Even though the Humane Society's webpage doesn't specifically frown on the idea, they do suggest that people "live peacefully with these animals," which likely precludes parachuting them into parts unknown.

BONUS FACT

Beavers build dams whenever they hear running water—even if the sound is synthetic. According to *DFW Urban Wildlife*, "a recording of running water was played in a field near a beaver pond. Despite the fact that it was on dry land, the beaver covered the tape player with branches and mud."

DAM IF YOU DO,
DAM IF YOU DON'T

The State of Michigan versus Beavers

If you're a homeowner, having a river or pond run through your property can be pretty cool. It can turn a rather nondescript piece of land into something more interesting and, with proper upkeep and safety, more fun. This is, of course, only true if the water was something you expected to be there. If, however, one day you wake up to find your typically dry backyard more akin to a bayou, that's a problem.

In 1997, when a homeowner in Montcalm County, Michigan, discovered unexpected water on his property, he went investigating. What—rather, who—he found was his neighbor Ryan DeVries. According to the Michigan Department of Environmental Quality (DEQ), DeVries had unlawfully diverted a waterway, causing flooding downstream. Specifically, the DEQ believed that DeVries had started to build wooden dams on a stream without a permit. The DEQ wrote him a letter, which outlined his allegedly unlawful activity and stated the fine of $10,000 per day for said crime.

However, there was a problem with this letter: Neither DeVries nor the man who owned the house he lived in, Stephen Tvedten, had built the dams. They were built by beavers. Tvedten decided to have fun with the DEQ, and wrote back: "A couple of beavers are in the (State unauthorized) process of constructing and maintaining two wood 'debris' dams across the outlet stream of my Spring Pond. While I did not pay for, nor authorize, their dam project, I think they would be highly offended you call their skillful use of natural building materials 'debris.'…I can safely state there is no dam way you could ever match their dam skills, their dam resourcefulness, their dam ingenuity, their dam persistence, their dam determination and/or their dam work ethic." The letter went on to defend the beavers' right to "dam legal representation."

The DEQ didn't find the response so funny. Instead, the agency doubled down, claiming they were fully aware the debris were beaver dams; the issue was that the beavers who built the dams had abandoned them long ago, but Mr. Tvedten had continued to maintain the dams. Tvedten countered by alleging that the reason the beavers had left the site was that the neighbor who was complaining about the flooding had killed them.

Regardless of what happened to the beavers, it was clear that Tvedten had probably not been maintaining their dams. And it was also clear that the absentee beavers were unlikely to reply to the DEQ's letter or apply for a permit. The DEQ dropped the investigation a few weeks later.

BONUS FACT

Beavers are mammals and are in the order Rodentia (as in "rodent"). Despite the fact that they're attracted to water and can swim pretty well, they're cousins of rats and mice—and are definitely not fish. But in the seventeenth century, when Europeans first came to the New World, this detail hardly mattered. According to an article in *Scientific American*, the Bishop of Quebec classified beavers as a fish, based on their habitat. As a result, "the general prohibition on the consumption of meat on Fridays did not apply to beaver meat."

THE SECRET LIFE OF F.D.C. WILLARD

*A Purr-fectly Good Way to
Make Your Editor Happy*

In the November 24, 1975, edition of the academic journal *Physical Review Letters*, there was a paper by two researchers titled "Two-, Three-, and Four-Atom Exchange Effects in bcc 3He." The authors of the paper were J.H. Hetherington and F.D.C. Willard, both identified as members of the Michigan State University physics department. Five years later, Professor Willard, showing that his expertise in that isotope of helium extended beyond the English language, published an article in a French science magazine on the antiferromagnetic properties of Helium-3. F.D.C. Willard was quite the scholar—and also a cat.

Willard (which wasn't his real name, as you'll learn about in more detail shortly) was owned by a human by the name of Professor Hetherington. Hetherington was, as his credentials *correctly* outlined, a physics professor at Michigan State, and he was the one who actually wrote both papers. And in almost all other situations, he would have been the sole author listed on the paper. But in this situation, there was a wrinkle in that plan.

Hetherington had written the first paper using "we" and "our" throughout, but before he submitted it, a colleague noted that the editors of *Physics Review Letters* frowned upon the use of plural first-person pronouns in papers with only one author. Changing all of these pronouns to "I"s and "my"s, unfortunately, was not as easy as a modern find-and-replace on the computer, as the word-processing technology during the time of his writing was the typewriter. Instead, Hetherington needed a collaborator to credit—something that was difficult, given that the paper was entirely his work.

As a solution to his predicament, Hetherington added his cat as the second author. F.D. stood for "Felis domesticus," the genus and species of the common house cat. The C stood for "Chester," the cat's actual name, and "Willard" was the name of the cat's father—the closest thing young Chester the cat had to a family name. Hetherington credited the fictitious professor Willard as a coauthor and positioned him as a colleague of his at Michigan State.

Ultimately, Hetherington did reveal his coauthor's true identity in 1978. The most commonly told story (recounted by organic chemistry professors Alex Nickon and Ernest F. Silversmith) is that he was effectively forced to do so when "a visitor came to campus to see Professor Hetherington, found him unavailable, and then asked to speak to Willard." He apparently was not sorry for his ruse, either, noting that most other scientists appreciated the humorous solution to his plural pronoun problem.

Willard, despite being a cat, wasn't done, though. A few years later, he "authored" another work, this time all on his own—and written in French! In 1980, Willard's byline graced an article in the French popular science magazine *La Recherche*. Of course, at this point the cat was out of the bag when it came to his identity. The real authors of the essay were a group of French and American scientists (including Hetherington). Creative differences over the content of the article resulted in none of them wanting their real name printed on it. Willard came to the rescue, taking credit once again.

BONUS FACT

The Helium-3 isotope has two protons and one neutron (the helium used for blowing up balloons, Helium-4, has two of each). In a fusion reaction combining two Helium-3 atoms, you end up with a Helium-4 atom and two extra protons. Those protons may be able to be used as a source of pollution-free, nonradioactive energy. There's one problem, however: Helium-3 is very rare on Earth. The good news (maybe)? It can be found in higher quantities on the Moon. As of 2007, people have been considering the viability of permanent, Moon-based Helium-3 farms.

WHEN THERE ARE TAXES TO PAY, THE CATS WON'T PLAY

*Why Cat Owners in Siberia Really
Need to Pay Their Taxes*

"[I]n this world," as the famous quote attributed to Benjamin Franklin goes, "nothing can be said to be certain, except death and taxes." And it's pretty much true: If you don't pay your taxes, the government will find a way to get the money you owe. In the United States, the penalties involved in this are typically a mix of more money owed (in the form of fines and interest) and, in egregious cases, prison time. And while the Internal Revenue Service (IRS) can get a lien on your home, it's rare that they'll foreclose. Instead, they often simply wait to collect the owed tax dollars until you sell your house or refinance your mortgage.

But what if you don't have anything of value? There are other tools available to the government, such as wage garnishment (when your employer diverts some percentage of your salary to the taxing authority per a court order). This way, the government gets what it is owed, and there's no opportunity for you to spend the money on something else before that happens.

While most countries have similar objectives when it comes to taxes, not all of them take the same approach when collecting these unpaid dues. In Russia, for example, many local governments will seize everyday items of value to make up for taxes owed by nonpayers (and just about anything you own is fair game). These items are held until the delinquent citizen pays off his or her tax bill.

That's exactly what happened in the Siberian city of Novosibirsk in December 2014. According to the BBC, a student in Novosibirsk owed about 12,000 rubles—about $200 US dollars—in taxes, but was unwilling or unable to pony up the cash. Bailiffs were dispatched to his residence to confiscate something of roughly the same value, to be held until the student could pay his societal debt. When the bailiffs arrived, however, they found nothing of similar value among the student's material possessions. That is until they expanded their search to include other items. Specifically, the bailiffs took notice of the student's cat, which was a British Shorthair. They realized it was a pedigreed cat and, therefore, was also expensive. The bailiffs seized the cat, holding it until the student could come up with the 12,000 rubles owed.

Apparently, pet-related tax seizure isn't an isolated incident in Siberia, either. At around the same time, bailiffs in another Russian town called Minusinsk seized the pets of a second tax delinquent. In this case (per Russian news agency Interfax) the pets held were a cat and a rabbit. Earlier that year, in the Siberian town of Tomsk, a businesswoman who owed 20,000 rubles found her four cats seized for nonpayment. Fortunately, despite being held for crimes they didn't commit, the pets were returned once their owners had paid the back taxes.

Cats and money are also linked in Russia in another way: through Sberbank, the largest bank in the nation. According to *Foreign Policy*, Russian superstition says that "it's good luck for the first creature to cross the threshold of a new home to be a feline." So, in August 2014, Sberbank began offering the opportunity for people to borrow a cat when they closed on a new house. Take out a mortgage and one of the Moscow branch's ten cats is yours—as a short-term rental, of course. The cat has to be returned within two hours.

THE CRULLER CRUSADERS

Why Cops Are Known for Eating Doughnuts

While most professions don't require twenty-four-hour, seven-days-a-week, three-hundred-sixty-five-days-a-year staffing, first responders are an exception. Emergencies and criminal activities can occur at any time of year, day or night, and they don't take time off, not even for Christmas. For this reason, there are always firefighters, EMTs, and police officers on duty at any given point in time. And police officers, unlike other emergency service providers, are often out on patrol at all hours of the day and night.

As you might imagine, this can be pretty boring. If you try driving around any given town at 3 a.m., you'll find that there isn't much to do. Even with the modern luxuries of self-serve gasoline, diners boasting late closing times, and twenty-four-hour drug stores, there aren't a lot of businesses open at this hour. And if you look further back at the 1950s, it was even rarer to find people hard at work during the dead of night. There was one notable exception, however: doughnut shops.

Most doughnuts—the light, airy, often glazed ones that you'll find at companies such as Krispy Kreme—are called "yeast doughnuts" because yeast causes them to rise. The rising process alone takes up to three hours. When you factor in the shaping, frying, glazing, optional jelly filling, and everything else involved in that delicious doughnut, the math paints a painstaking picture. Want to have fresh doughnuts ready for the first wave of office workers at about 6 a.m.? You'll basically need to work through the night. "Cake doughnuts," like apple cider doughnuts or the all-chocolate doughnuts you can get at most shops, take less time because they use baking powder and/or baking soda to rise the batter instantly as it cooks. However, most good doughnut shops will have both types, so regardless of the wonders of baking powder and baking soda, you'll still be up late. And if you're going to be at work overnight anyway, why not open up to customers?

For police officers working night shifts, this was pretty convenient. Driving around town, a brightly lit doughnut shop sign promising a snack, much-needed coffee, and a place to take a bathroom break was a welcome sight. And for the doughnut shop employees themselves, having officers stop by—and ideally hang out in the parking lot for a while—was great. There weren't a lot of potential customers in the wee hours of the night, but the nature of the business (specifically during a time before credit cards) meant that these eateries often had a lot of cash on hand, making them an obvious target for crime. The cop/doughnut relationship was symbiotic.

It did, however, get out of control after a while. According to *Atlas Obscura*, by the 1960s, coffee shops would give free or significantly discounted doughnuts to officers in hopes of enticing them to swing by often, especially overnight. In 1964, a cop journal called *Police* spelled out explicitly why officers should refuse these free or discounted items: "Do not accept gifts—donuts and coffee. This gives the impression of partiality." But this warning hasn't stopped the practice—who would turn down a free cruller?—and the legendary love affair between police officers and the round, fried pastry continues on.

BONUS FACT

The New York City Police Department used to issue officers an 11" baton for their daily patrols and then upgrade them to a 26" version for when they made rounds after dark (this accounted for the increased risk of danger). The latter were informally called "nightsticks" for this reason—a term now used to describe most police batons.

CALLING IN THE B TEAM

The Police Officer Whose Job Is a Buzz

As of 2018, there were approximately 35,000 police officers in the New York City Police Department. These NYPD officers serve many different roles; there is a bomb squad, an anti-gang unit, a team focused on drug infractions, another team that deals only with public transportation, and, of course, a counterterrorism unit. Many other officers are more generalists, assigned to an area—a "precinct"—and expected to cover a variety of issues.

However, what unit you are in doesn't necessarily dictate what job you fill. Similarly, your home precinct may not be the only place you work. For these types of jobs—the ones that require a special hand—the NYPD may call in the B Team. Or, more accurately, the "bee" team. Yes, the NYPD has an on-staff *beekeeper*. Two, actually, and the role hasn't been without the buzz of controversy over its nearly twenty-five years.

The role began in February 1994, when an officer named Anthony Planakis applied to join the force. He listed a curious hobby on his resume: He was an avid beekeeper. As Planakis told NPR, beekeeping was in his blood; he was a fourth-generation beekeeper, himself having first engaged with the buzzing insects in 1977. Surprisingly, this hobby came in handy nearly immediately when his sergeant assigned him to wrangle some bees in Harlem just weeks after he took the job. By the winter of 1995, he was the department's unofficial beekeeper, taking on the nickname "Tony Bees."

For nearly twenty years, Planakis was the on-call guy whenever a New Yorker called the police to deal with a bee infestation. However, the unofficial position came with a problem: ambiguity. When Planakis removed hordes of bees from afflicted homes and businesses and their surroundings, those bees became the property of the NYPD. But, as Planakis told *Gothamist*, it wasn't clear what he should do with those bees, as "there was no one else qualified to handle [the bees] and no procedure in place" for their relocation. Planakis claims that he'd give the bees to beekeepers he knew without taking any remuneration from them.

Unfortunately, many at the NYPD didn't believe him, instead accusing him of either keeping the bees for himself (he had his own hive from which he harvested honey) or selling them to friends. Planakis vehemently denied this and the police department never investigated him, but the damage was done. He left the force in 2014, telling the media that this undue scrutiny from superiors pushed him into early retirement—although he does come back on occasion to help out with an errant swarm or two.

While the department originally intended to retire the unofficial beekeeper role after Planakis left, plans changed in early 2015. The department instead decided to formalize the position. That summer, it named a counterterrorism detective, Daniel Higgins, and a Queens police officer, Darren Mays, as co-beekeepers. The NYPD has resolved the ambiguities that ended Planakis's career early; as the *New York Post* reported, "Higgins and Mays aren't paid extra for their beekeeping duties, but they get to keep the bees for their own use."

BONUS FACT

Bumblebees are quite deserving of their name: They tend to bumble a lot, colliding into things often. Per *Gizmodo*, "bumblebees actually bump into things pretty frequently—around once per second." But it's not their fault, *Gizmodo* explains: "It's not that they're bad at flying, but that the air around them tends to move unpredictably."

MANHATTAN'S INVISIBLE WALL

*The Wire That Lets Jewish Residents
Carry on Carrying*

If you live in certain areas—New York City, for example—it's probably not a great idea to look up at the sky as you walk up the streets and avenues. But if you do, assuming you don't bump into anyone, you may notice something: a faint line shooting off lampposts, power line poles, and other tall roadside structures. That line is actually a wire, and it's the border of an otherwise invisible wall around most of Manhattan.

To fully understand, you need to learn a bit about Judaism: The Sabbath—Friday night and Saturday—is intended to be a day of rest. That means you don't do any work, which here can be defined in ways that aren't immediately obvious to those of other faiths. For example, starting a fire, writing something down, tearing an object, and carrying something from one area to another. A prohibition on carrying seems sensible here: If you're supposed to be resting, you probably shouldn't be lugging objects home from work anyway.

But there are two important things to note here. First, the ban on carrying isn't focused only on large, heavy items; it's universal, meaning you can't carry anything. That said, the ban isn't on carrying altogether, just on carrying between two different areas. You can carry a glass of water from the sink to the table—that's all within your house—but you can't carry that same glass of water from the privacy of your home to somewhere public.

This rule causes problems, however. Let's say you were on your way to synagogue on Saturday morning. You probably want to lock the doors to your house behind you and now have house keys that you need to take with you. Carrying your keys is a violation of the rule. So, a creative solution was in order. And that solution is called an eruv.

An eruv—"ay-roov"—is the invisible wall. Basically, the community gets together and agrees on an entire neighborhood that is one private domain, letting those observing the Sabbath carry items around this neighborhood as if they were in their own home. Eruvs are very common, at least in areas like New York City with a high density of observant Jewish residents.

But if you're a believer who cares about the eruv from a religious perspective, whether the community *has* an eruv isn't the end of the story. Even though the "wall" is primarily ritual, it still exists in tangible form—and those who observe take this seriously. If the wire isn't up, the wall isn't either. This can be hard to keep track of—the Manhattan eruv, for example, is miles long, which is way too much for any one person to monitor. As a result, the community runs a website with a status indicator displayed prominently.

BONUS FACT

Another invisible feature of New York City? The anti-theft features built into the light bulbs in the subways. The city's transit system uses light bulbs with left-handed threaded screws in order to prevent theft. Instead of turning them to the left to loosen them, you need to turn them to the right. Sure, once you learn this, you can still steal the light bulbs, but they won't work at your home. As subway history website NYCSubway.org explains, "Vandals who didn't know this were surprised when they found that they would not screw into ordinary light fixtures."

WHEN THE LAW STEPS IN, SOMETIMES MAPS MAKE LESS SENSE

Why Long Island Isn't Always an Island

Long Island juts out of the southeast corner of New York State, serving as a barrier between the Atlantic Ocean, Connecticut, and Westchester County, New York. It's home to two boroughs of New York City (Queens and Brooklyn) as well as two of the state's other counties (Nassau and Suffolk). It is both the longest (118 miles) and largest (1,401 square miles) island in the contiguous United States and has a population of more than 7.5 million people. It's also larger than Rhode Island, and if it were a state, its population would place it among the fifteen largest in America. It truly is a long island. Legally, however, it's not always an "island." And that's the way New York prefers it.

In 1985, the US Supreme Court ruled in a case titled United States v. Maine (which is an odd name for a case focusing on Long Island and Rhode Island). The issue in front of the court was whether the federal government or the relevant state governments had jurisdiction over all of the little bits of the Atlantic

Ocean coastline that are sheltered by islands. Thirteen different Atlantic states were defendants in the lawsuit brought by the federal government, and as Maine is the most geographically northern of those states, its name is in the case caption. By the time the court ruled on the matter, however, there were only two areas of interest: Long Island and Rhode Island's Block Island.

In front of the case was the application of an international agreement called the Convention on the Territorial Sea and the Contiguous Zone. In it is the issue that shorelines aren't typically straight lines. There are, as the convention notes, places "where the coastline is deeply indented and cut into," and the convention allows nations to claim those bodies (called "juridical bays") as part of their territory as if they were lakes. That is, these bays aren't included when measuring the distance from the shore when trying to determine where international waters begin.

Normally, national governments therefore want to claim that these bodies of water are simple indentations, as doing so extends the nation's reach farther into the ocean. But "islands may not normally be considered extensions of the mainland for purposes of creating juridical bays," as the Supreme Court noted. And if Long Island Sound wasn't a juridical bay, it would be a "territorial water" and therefore under control of the federal government.

New York, wanting to maintain control over Long Island Sound—there's revenue attached, after all—fought back. The state thus came up with a clever argument: Despite its name and its clear geography, Long Island shouldn't be considered an "island." And the court agreed. The 9-0 opinion notes that "the East River, which separates Long Island from the mainland and from Manhattan Island, was at one time as shallow as 15 to 18 feet" and the river itself is "not an opening to the sea." As a result, the court found, "Long Island functions as an extension of the mainland"—more like a peninsula than an island.

Block Island, on the other hand, remained an island. The straight line the court drew to divide between the juridical bay and territorial waters ran to Block Island's west, putting the little piece of Rhode Island clearly out in the high seas.

BONUS FACT

If you're driving in Long Island during the day, you won't find any construction happening on state highways—and you can thank radio superstar Howard Stern for that. In 1994, Stern announced that his intention to run for Governor of New York on a three-pronged platform: reinstatement of the death penalty (which he later changed his mind about), removal of highway tolls, and a law that would get rid of road repairs during peak traffic periods. He withdrew well before election day but was still somewhat successful; in 1995, New York passed the "Howard Stern Bill," which limited road construction on state roads to overnight hours.

WHEN TRASH GOES DOWN THE TUBES

The Island with No Garbage

If you walk around the island of Manhattan long enough, you'll certainly come across heaps of garbage bags piled up on street curbs. With more than two million people living on the island and another nearly two million entering each day to work and play, there's a lot of trash to be collected. Building management, superintendents, and janitorial crews put the garbage out on the sidewalk so that sanitation workers can drive by and easily toss the refuse into the back of their trucks. This is not surprising, though. How else could Manhattan deal with garbage?

Well, it turns out that some of Manhattan has a very different solution. Roosevelt Island sits in the East River, with the island of Manhattan to its west and Long Island to its east. This 2-mile-long, 800-foot-wide strip of land is home to approximately ten thousand New Yorkers. Like its neighbor to the west, Roosevelt Island is part of the borough of Manhattan. Unlike the more famous part of the borough, though, Roosevelt Island has almost no garbage trucks. To understand why you'll need to look to Walt Disney World.

When Walt Disney came up with his plan for a magical city in Orlando, Florida, he had a grand desire to make it something beyond what anyone had seen before. Having garbage on the roadside as Mickey and friends paraded down Main Street, U.S.A. would be the opposite of that, so the Disney team sought other solutions. What they found was a Swedish company's innovation, called the Automated Vacuum Collection system, or AVAC for short.

AVAC is a series of interconnected, underground pneumatic tubes. At this time, trash chutes were already common throughout the United States, particularly in larger buildings, and AVAC used the same basic idea. However, instead of that trash collecting into a dumpster or trash compactor, the high-powered vacuums in the AVAC would fly the garbage off to a centralized location away from the theme park's guests.

No trash bags on the street and no garbage trucks blocking traffic—sounds great, right? The Swedish innovators thought so, and the company wasn't intent on letting Disney keep this technology to itself, either. They believed that it was so transformative (cities without garbage trucks!) that it would sweep the nation. Unfortunately, things didn't play out this way, but there's one other place that did welcome the AVAC system: Roosevelt Island.

For most of its history, the island was mainly used to house hospitals and an asylum (called "the New York City Lunatic Asylum" until 1894), and few people outside of these institutions lived on the island full-time. But an effort to increase affordable housing in the city in the 1970s changed Roosevelt Island's character: State and federal grants funded the creation of apartment buildings there, as well as an above-water tramway connecting it to Manhattan Island.

When these new buildings were created, they were done so in a way that minimized the need for cars—which included garbage trucks, so installing the AVAC system made a lot of sense. So if you are on Roosevelt Island, you won't see a lot of trash or trash collectors. Instead, as *The New York Times* so nicely put it, there's "a 1,000-horsepower vacuum...silently sucking garbage from their buildings at 60 miles per hour."

BONUS FACT

Like Roosevelt Island and Walt Disney World, Taiwan doesn't want garbage piling up on the streets. Unlike these locations, however, Taiwan doesn't have an AVAC system. Their trick? They copied ice-cream trucks. Residents in Taiwan don't leave their trash on the curb for pickup; instead, the trash collectors come at prescheduled times, and the residents bring their garbage right to the truck. To make sure they know the trucks are coming, *HuffPost* notes, "garbage trucks, like ice cream vans, are equipped with speakers that play music" designed to alert residents that their pickup time has come.

THE PRESIDENT'S SECRET TRAIN STATION

How to Sneak POTUS Out of New York City

Forty-four platforms and sixty-seven tracks make Grand Central Terminal, located in the heart of Midtown Manhattan, the largest train station in the world. And that number doesn't even account for a secret platform (it would hardly be a secret in that case) with a very special purpose: escape.

Grand Central opened its doors in 1871. While the building itself stretches from 42nd to 45th Street, the terminal as a whole extends underground as far uptown as 50th Street. One of the buildings above these tracks, located between 49th and 50th Streets, was once a powerhouse for the terminal. The powerhouse had its own loading platform beneath it, used for discharging workers and transporting machinery to the site as needed. However, when Con Edison, the local utility company, began to provide power to the terminal, the powerhouse became redundant. And by the late 1920s, the world-famous Waldorf Astoria Hotel took over the entire block between 49th and 50th Streets, bulldozing the powerhouse but—for reasons unknown—keeping its access to the underground railway. By historical accident, the Waldorf Astoria now had its own, though rarely used, train station.

Rarely—but not never, to be clear. When the President of the United States is in town, the platform, known as Track 61, is a backdoor to safety. For decades, the Waldorf Astoria has played host to presidents visiting the city, and the secret platform has certainly come in handy (the tradition for presidents to check into the Waldorf Astoria may have even stemmed from Track 61's existence). Legend has it that when Franklin Delano Roosevelt visited the hotel in the mid-1940s, he employed a custom-made train car that brought him right to the hotel's "secret" train platform. It is believed that this was for reasons of both vanity (he wanted to hide the fact that he was wheelchair-bound) and security. His custom-made car—outfitted with gun ports and plate armor—still sits on the tracks, somewhere beneath Grand Central, as it is too large to move without taking it apart. It also remains on site because it may prove useful in the future. When President George W. Bush gave an address to the United Nations General Assembly in 2003, he also chose the Waldorf Astoria specifically because of Track 61; per MSNBC, as Bush rested and prepared in the hotel above, a train sat idly below, "ready to whisk him to safety at a moment's notice in the event of a terrorist attack." (It's unclear if Bush's train was the very same used by FDR.)

Despite being dubbed a "secret," however, the track appears on blueprints of Grand Central Terminal that are available to the public. On occasion, the transit authority will even give the press a private tour of FDR's old train and its surrounding areas. There are no public tours unfortunately, but you can still see the train car if you're lucky enough: Some regular commuter trains pass by it on their way into and out of Grand Central. All you need to do is be on that train looking out an eastside window at the right time to catch a glimpse. Or you could just become the president.

BONUS FACT

In the 1936 Olympics in Berlin, African-American athlete Jesse Owens famously won four gold medals—a huge accomplishment that debunked, in front of the whole world and Hitler's supporters, the idea that Aryans were genetically superior to other races. When Owens arrived back in the United States, he was greeted like a hero. New York City hosted a ticker-tape parade in his honor, after which he was received as the guest of honor at a reception at the Waldorf Astoria. Despite this, however, he wasn't allowed to use the main entrance at the hotel. Due to the hotel's discriminatory policies at the time, Owens had to use a back entrance and take a service elevator to the party.

SKIRTING THE RULES

The Short Reason for Swedish Skirts

In politics, things can get weird. Take, for example, the 2018 Democratic primary election for the New York gubernatorial nomination. As the summer came to a close, former *Sex and the City* actor and political activist Cynthia Nixon challenged incumbent Andrew Cuomo (she was ultimately unsuccessful) and the two sparred over the ground rules for their debate. Team Nixon sent a seemingly odd request to WCBS-TV, the media company that was running the event: They asked that the temperature at the venue, an auditorium at Hofstra University, be set to exactly 76°F.

But the request isn't all that strange. Men, on average, like their workplaces a bit cooler than women do. There are a lot of factors that may play into why this is true. One is physiologies; according to a 1998 study by researchers at the University of Utah, "women had a mean core temperature of 97.8 degrees Fahrenheit compared with 97.4 for men," but "hand temperature for women was 87.2, while men recorded 90.0 degrees." A second reason behind why men may like cooler office temperatures, at least in warmer weather, is their typical attire; while women have workplace clothing options such as light dresses or skirts, dress codes rarely allow men to opt for shorts over pants.

In a workplace where temperatures rarely go above 76°F, this may seem like no big deal. Sure, it can be a bit uncomfortable to manipulate spreadsheets or navigate a conference call when it's on the warm side, but you probably won't break a sweat. But when you work outside of a temperature-regulated office—on a train, for example—warm days can lead to very hot working conditions.

This is the problem for many of Sweden's train operators and staff. When it is in the mid-70s outside, it approaches 90°F in the train cabins. For the female employees, this is not great, but at least they can wear lighter skirts to help combat the heat. And before 2013, the male employees could wear shorts, which also helped. But that January, their company, Roslagståg AB, was acquired by another, named Arriva, which instituted a more formal dress code. From that point on, shorts weren't allowed.

But the dress code didn't mandate pants for male employees— and this created a neat loophole.

That summer, a dozen male train drivers decided to protest the shorts ban by wearing skirts to work. They weren't aiming to make a political point, but the potential for discrimination claims was certainly a weapon they had at the ready. A spokesperson for Arriva realized this right away, telling the local press that "one should look decent and proper when representing Arriva and the present uniforms do that," and that "If the man only wants [to wear] a skirt then that is okay" as "[t]o tell them to do something else would be discrimination." If drivers—male or female— wanted to wear skirts, they were welcome to do so.

The company had seemingly called their bluff, and a battle of wills—or perhaps more accurately, exposed knees—ensued. For two weeks, if the weather wasn't cool enough to warrant wearing long pants, the twelve protestors donned skirts to work, walking up the aisles collecting tickets to the wayward looks and whispered comments made by riders. Their point sufficiently made, Arriva reversed their decision and reinstated the ability to wear shorts during warmer weather.

BONUS FACT

This successful protest couldn't have happened in New York City, at least not today. In December 2015, the city's Commission on Human Rights issued guidance around the city's anti-discrimination law. Per the city's website, employers can run afoul of the law by "enforcing dress codes, uniforms, and grooming standards that impose different requirements based on sex or gender," including "enforcing a policy that requires men to wear ties or women to wear skirts."

TO BOLDLY GO WHERE NO COUPLE HAS GONE BEFORE

A First Kiss That Was Out of This World

In the future, men will wear skirts—well, that is if Star Trek is predictive of the future. In the first season of *Star Trek: The Next Generation*, male background characters can occasionally be seen wearing one-piece dresses with skirts that end above the knee. In one episode ("Liaisons," season seven, episode two), an officer is even admonished for complaining about having to wear "ridiculous uniforms" that "look like dresses." His commanding officer chastises him for having an "incredibly outmoded and sexist attitude."

For Star Trek fans, this exchange likely didn't feel out of place; it was hardly the first time the franchise made an effort to represent certain ideals. The most famous? A kiss—one that only happened due to a mutiny.

The original *Star Trek* series starred William Shatner, a Caucasian man, as Captain James T. Kirk. Among Kirk's officers was Lieutenant Nyota Uhura, portrayed by African-American actress Nichelle Nichols. In season three, episode ten ("Plato's Stepchildren"), the crew finds themselves being held hostage on an alien planet whose inhabitants have psychokinetic powers that allow them to make people do whatever they want.

For reasons only clear to their captors, four members of the *Enterprise* crew are coupled off. Both couples, Kirk and Uhura being one of them, are forced to kiss against their will. Today, few viewers would care, but at the time the episode aired, this event was a big deal. Few interracial kisses had been portrayed on TV before, and this was almost certainly the first time a Caucasian man and an African-American woman had kissed on TV.

And network executives weren't happy about it. Given the cultural backdrop of the time, executives at NBC, the company that aired *Star Trek*, feared backlash. They tried to convince the showrunners to come up with a less controversial solution. One idea was to have Spock, Kirk's half-alien second-in-command, be the one to embrace Uhura; the theory was that viewers wouldn't be as upset because while Spock was also Caucasian, he was also seen as a nonhuman. Shatner refused, wanting to stick to the original script. The executives came up with a new idea: Film two versions, one with a kiss, and one with a hug. Later, they would decide which one to use.

Shatner and Nichols had no choice; while the promise to decide later was likely an empty one, there wasn't room for argument. So the cast and crew shot takes of both versions. It looked like the kiss wouldn't make it to the screen after all.

But it did, as time would tell. Why? Because when the editors reviewed the footage, they realized that in the nonkiss versions, Shatner and Nichols were working against the will of the network executives: They had intentionally flubbed every shot. For example, as Nichols wrote in her autobiography, "the last shot, which looked okay on the set, actually had Bill wildly crossing his eyes. It was so corny and just plain bad it was unusable." NBC had a choice: Cut the scene entirely (and ruin the episode) or go with the kiss version and take the risk. They chose the latter.

And the anticipated backlash? It never came. Per Nichols's book, there was only one letter complaining, and it was arguably more supportive than not. It stated, "I am totally opposed to the mixing of the races. However, any time a red-blooded American boy like Captain Kirk gets a beautiful dame in his arms that looks like Uhura, he ain't gonna fight it."

BONUS FACT

The famous catchphrase, "Beam me up, Scotty!," isn't an accurate quote; at no point during the original TV series or movies did Captain Kirk ever utter this exact phrase. He did come close in one episode ("This Side of Paradise") when he said "beam me up," but he did not mention Scotty. In the movie *Star Trek IV: The Journey Home*, he says "Scotty, beam me up!"—closer, but still no cigar.

THE NEGRO MOTORIST GREEN BOOK

How African-American Motorists Drove Around Jim Crow

Every year, Zagat publishes a series of guides to the restaurants in virtually every major city in the United States. The guides feature short, curated descriptions of each eatery, touching upon the must-try (or must-avoid) dishes, service, decor, and of course, prices. But what Zagat doesn't tell you is if the restaurant will serve you if you're African American.

There's a good reason for that: For more than fifty years, it's been illegal for a restaurant in the United States to refuse service to a customer on the basis of his or her race. Before this legislation, however, traveling through certain parts of the country was difficult for African-American citizens, as finding a place to eat or sleep that would accept their business was a challenge. Fortunately, one man took a lead in solving this issue. The result: *The Negro Motorist Green Book*.

In 1932, an African-American postal worker named Victor H. Green came up with the idea for a guidebook that would detail the businesses that welcomed African-American travelers. Green's first edition, which came out four years later in 1936, focused on restaurants and hotels in the New York City area, as that's where he lived and had firsthand knowledge of where he was and wasn't welcome due to his race.

The guide proved popular, so Green looked to expand its reach. He asked his readers to send in tips on other businesses; any accepted tip earned the correspondent $1. By 1941, Green had upped the bounty to $5 per accepted tip. He also asked his fellow postal workers to help research. According to *The New York Times*, many mail carriers would "ask around on their routes" in furtherance of Greens's efforts. His plan succeeded: As CNN explains, with these tips, the guide "eventually expanded to include everything from lodging and gas stations to tailor shops and doctors' offices across the nation, as well as in Bermuda, Mexico, and Canada."

Beyond being a boon for those facing discrimination, the *Green Book* was a commercial success. Many African American–friendly businesses advertised in it. Esso, a precursor brand to ExxonMobil, was a particularly important advertiser: Not only was this chain a financial supporter of the *Green Book*, but it was also a major distributor of it. Esso was also one of the few companies at this time that allowed African Americans to become franchisees.

Before the 1940s were over, *The Negro Motorist Green Book* had become a must-have guide for tens of thousands of African-American travelers, to the benefit of the larger community as well.

And for an even better reason than anyone could have hoped for: The *Green Book* no longer exists. With the passing of the Civil Rights Act of 1964, it became effectively obsolete, with Green publishing the final edition in 1966.

BONUS FACT

Martin Luther King Jr. and his wife, Coretta Scott, were married on June 18, 1953—but their honeymoon wasn't spent at a hotel, as the ones in their region did not accept African-American guests. According to the book *The Wisdom of Martin Luther King, Jr.*, the two spent their first evening together as husband and wife at a funeral home.

WE'RE (NOT) ALL EARS

What Goes Wrong When You Use Your Eyes to Hear

When you attend a live show, your eyes are focused on whatever is transpiring on the stage in front of you. While the actors are performing, the rest of the room is dark and there isn't much else to grab your attention. In many cases, the only exception is a bit of light in the center of the room, right in front of the stage. This light is from the lamp of the orchestral conductor, who is leading a team of talented musicians. As part of the audience, you don't see the harpsichordist, percussionist, or any of the other music makers in this team, though: They're hidden in a darkened orchestra pit.

And that's okay. After all, what the orchestra *looks* like isn't important: The music speaks for itself. However, before the late twentieth century, it often didn't. Instead, the eyes trumped the ears when it came to orchestral auditions.

Let's say you're a world-class violinist trying out for a nearby city's symphony orchestra. Nowadays, when you arrive to the audition, you won't introduce yourself to the panel or otherwise greet them. In fact, you won't even see them—or more to the point, *they* won't see *you*. You walk into the room and sit down behind a screen. The evaluators will hear your work but can't see your face (or anything else about you).

The reason for this seemingly odd way of auditioning? Bias. The orchestral world is quite small, and you don't want evaluators giving an advantage, even subconsciously, to their friends or acquaintances who may also be auditioning. It's the music itself that truly matters, after all. In the 1970s and 1980s, orchestras began this practice of obscuring the identity of prospective members as much as possible. And while wanting to avoid favoring friends may have been the thrust of the change, it revealed something else: a significant gender bias.

In 1997, a team of researchers published a paper via the National Bureau of Economic Research titled "Orchestrating Impartiality: The Impact of 'Blind' Auditions on Female Musicians." As the abstract notes, "female musicians in the top five symphony orchestras in the United States were less than 5 percent of all players in 1970 but are 25 percent [in 1997]." This is a huge shift, and the researchers dug deeper into the data to see if it was a coincidence, or if the modern, more anonymous way of screening caused the increase. What they found was that "the screen increases by 50 percent the probability a woman will be advanced out of certain preliminary rounds" and "the switch to 'blind' auditions can explain between 25 percent and 46 percent of the increase in the percentage female in the orchestras since 1970."

In the music world, though, the role of gender bias in auditions hasn't exactly been a secret, and the screen placed between auditioning musicians and panelists wasn't the only innovation aimed at reducing that bias. Women also realized at this time that their shoes—even unseen—could give away their gender; the sound heels make when a musician walks into an audition is something that some panelists are sure to pick up on even subconsciously.

As a result, many women began wearing flats to auditions. Fortunately, the orchestras themselves also began to take on the task of hiding the sound of a person's steps. Today, if you're auditioning, chances are you're not only going to be sitting behind a screen, but you'll also be walking across a carpeted runway to get to your seat.

BONUS FACT

Before the mid-1990s, the Vienna Philharmonic Orchestra—widely regarded as one of the world's best—refused to admit women as members. That changed in February 1997, just before the orchestra was scheduled to perform at New York's Carnegie Hall. Fearing protestors, a majority of the orchestra voted to make harpist Anna Lelkes a full member. Lelkes wasn't difficult for the VPO to find, either; she had been playing with the orchestra regularly as an adjunct member for twenty-six years, despite never receiving the same pay as members, nor appearing in the group's annual photos.

A WORKING WOMAN'S DAY OFF

The General Strikes That—Generally—Worked

On Friday, October 24, 1975, something strange happened in Iceland—or, more accurately, *nothing* happened, strangely. Telephone calls failed to connect. Newspapers didn't go to print. Theaters didn't open. Schools, by and large, also closed their doors for the day, as did banks and factories. Flights were canceled across the nation. Iceland, figuratively speaking, was frozen in place.

The cause was Kvennafrídagurinn, translated in English: "Women's Day Off." The United Nations had declared that year "International Women's Year" and planned a number of conferences in support of this effort. These conferences were largely antiseptic and boring, however, and when five of Iceland's women's rights organizations got together to figure out how to activate International Women's Year in their own country, one had a much grander idea. They proposed that women declare a general strike instead. For one day, women would be encouraged to take the day off: They wouldn't go to work, they would have their husbands watch the kids—generally speaking, they would pretend they weren't even there. As *The New York Times* reported, the goal of the "Day Off" was to "show that women are indispensable to the country's economic and national life"—assuming, that is, that Icelandic women actually participated in the event.

Leading up to the day itself, many Icelandic men didn't think much of it, *The New York Times* recounts. They "treated [it] as a joke when it was first suggested." This would prove to be a mistake, though, as a staggering 90 percent of Iceland's women decided to join the protest, with many attending rallies across the small island nation. Per the BBC, the largest protest of the day—which took place in the capital, Reykjavik—drew approximately 25,000 people. This was a significantly large number given that there were only about 220,000 total people living in Iceland at the time. The events of the day did not disappoint, either. The 25,000 strong were met with inspiring speakers (including two members of the legislature), songs of solidarity, and discussions on how to bring gender equality into the forefront of the Icelandic conversation.

And as it turned out, the protests did exactly that, because they brought the country to a halt. Not only did businesses across Iceland shut down, but the strike also affected childcare and housework. Mothers throughout the island left the care of their children to the fathers, which meant kids were brought along to work with their dads. Many men, frustrated with how difficult it was to get work done while also watching a child, dubbed the event "The Long Friday." The efforts—or lack thereof—of these women certainly did not go unnoticed.

The protest also brought about permanent change. The next year, Iceland passed a law that guaranteed equal rights regardless of gender. And in 1980, the country elected Vigdís Finnbogadóttir as its fourth president. Vigdís was the world's first woman democratically elected to lead her country.

BONUS FACT

Yes, "Vigdís" is the correct way to refer to Vigdís Finnbogadóttir, assuming you don't want to spell out (or attempt to pronounce) her entire name every time. This is because Icelandic names aren't like those in the rest of the Western world. Last names in Iceland aren't family names that are consistent from generation to generation (changes via marriage notwithstanding); they're patronymic, which means they're based on a male ancestor. In this case, the name is based on her father's first name. Vigdís's father's full name was Finnbogi Rútur Þorvaldsson; Finnbogadóttir translates to "daughter of Finnbogi."

MAYBE YOU *SHOULD* LISTEN TO YOUR MOTHER

The Woman Who Got Women the Vote

Today, the idea that the right to vote should be restricted to only men is absurd. Yet, not very long ago, this was the reality for US women. In fact, the United States Constitution didn't afford women the right to vote until 1920. Since then, women (and men) have celebrated this historical event by going to Rochester, New York, and sticking their "I Voted!" stickers on the gravestone of famous women's suffragist, Susan B. Anthony. But they should also be thanking lesser-known Phoebe Ensminger Burn.

The process for amending the Constitution is quite cumbersome, requiring either a constitutional convention or a two-thirds vote by both houses of Congress. And once it is past that hurdle, at least three quarters of the states need to ratify the amendment. Congress sent the Nineteenth Amendment guaranteeing women the right to vote to the states for ratification on June 4, 1919. A year later, it had the support of thirty states—one fewer than it needed to become part of the Constitution (there were forty-eight states at this time). The success of the proposed amendment was in doubt. Eight of the remaining thirteen states rejected the measure before August 1920; the governors of a few others refused to even consider holding a session to address the question. In August 1920, Tennessee's legislature finally decided to hold its vote—one that would likely decide the fate of the amendment.

The Tennessee senate voted to ratify with relative ease, but the state's house had more difficulty with the decision. Anti-suffrage legislators wanted to set aside the issue for another time (or never), so they proposed to table the measure. However, this vote resulted in a 48-48 tie. They would have to vote on the issue. By this point, observers and legislators alike knew that the outcome wasn't good for the suffrage movement. Not only had the last vote resulted in a tie, but both legislators and supporters had taken to wearing their stance on their lapels—literally. Pro-suffrage voters donned yellow roses; anti-suffragists countered by wearing red roses. And when the measure came up for a vote, there were forty-eight legislators wearing yellow roses and forty-eight wearing red ones.

Then, however, something odd happened: One legislator flipped his vote, shocking all who were watching. Despite the fact that he was wearing a red rose *and* had voted to table the amendment just days earlier, twenty-five-year-old Harry T. Burn voted "aye" (yes) for the ratification. The credit for his last-minute switch? His mother, the aforementioned Phoebe Ensminger Burn. After news of the motion to table the issue spread, Mrs. Burn wrote a seven-page letter to her son—one he clenched in his hands as he cast the decisive vote. At the end of the letter she wrote, "Hurray and vote for Suffrage and don't keep them in doubt. I noticed [anti-suffragist legislator Walter] Chandlers' speech, it was very bitter. I've been waiting to see how you stood but have not seen anything yet...." Harry Burns did what his mother asked, and with that the Nineteenth Amendment became part of the Constitution.

The last European nation to grant women the right to vote was Liechtenstein, in 1984. It was the fourth time the nation offered a referendum on women's suffrage, and it was a close call, with 2,370 votes in favor and 2,251 against. Like the attempts in 1971 and 1973, only men were allowed to vote, but the first attempt in 1968 was different. Women were allowed to vote, and more women (2,507) cast ballots than men (2,228). Despite this, the ballot measure failed. Eight hundred eighty-seven men voted for suffrage and 1,341 against. Women, on the other hand, were almost evenly divided: 1,268 voted for, but 1,241 voted against.

A POLITICAL KNOCKOUT

The Black Day of the Indiana General Assembly

As the United States Constitution was originally written, the election of US senators was done by state governments. Specifically, Article I, Section 3 of the Constitution gave state legislatures the power to elect the person to fill that office. The framers of the Constitution did not want populism to take root and saw this indirect way of electing leaders as a hedge against that outcome. Today, this thought seems ridiculous—but it took a brawl in the Indiana statehouse to come to that conclusion.

The story begins in the early 1870s with the presiding state senator, Republican Isaac P. Gray, pushing Indiana to ratify Constitutional amendments that outlawed slavery and granted African Americans the right to vote. The Democrats in the chamber were against these measures and tried to deny the chamber a quorum by refusing to be present for the vote. Gray locked the doors so the Democrats couldn't leave, and they responded by hiding in a cloak closet. Gray figured that this was close enough: He had the clerk mark the Democrats as present and record their votes as abstentions. Indiana ratified the amendments.

Gray, though, wasn't long for the Republican Party, which many saw as marred by corruption. He and others tried to form a new party, but he eventually realized this splinter effort would fail. Instead, he became a Democrat, winning the 1876, 1880, and 1884 elections for governor, with Mahlon D. Mason as his running mate the latter year. Two years later, a US Senate seat opened up and Gray wanted it. Some of the Democrats, still miffed about Gray's coup a decade earlier, tried to block his election, convincing Mason to resign from office. Then, instead of arguing that Gray wouldn't be a good choice for senator, they now argued that Gray *couldn't* be made a senator as there was no one to take his place as governor. To solve this problem, a special election was held in 1886 to fill the role. Republican Robert S. Robertson won. The Democrats' plan had backfired. Republicans were now in favor of Gray's election: If Gray were to get the Senate seat, Robertson would become governor. The Democrats then sued to prevent Robertson from being seated, arguing that the special election was unconstitutional. The Indiana Supreme Court disagreed, ruling that Robertson was the rightful seatholder.

Yet it didn't end there. On February 24, 1887, Robertson showed up at the state's senate for his first day as lieutenant governor and was physically attacked and ejected by some of the Democrats. The senate president temporarily ordered the doors locked, and the two parties came to blows. The fight only ended when a senate Democrat took out a gun and fired it toward the ceiling. However, news of the unrest had already reached the other chamber in the legislature. There, hundreds of Republicans swarmed the building, dragging Democrats outside. Eventually, after four hours of fighting, the police intervened. The brawl was dubbed the "Black Day of the Indiana General Assembly" by the media.

Robertson never was seated. After the imbroglio, the Republican-controlled house and Democratic-controlled senate refused to work with one another, and the legislative session came to a de facto close. The violence did lead to positive change, however, albeit indirectly. The framers' original thesis—that when electing US senators, state legislators would act with a higher degree of sophistication than everyday voters—no longer seemed so credible. Over the next thirty years, efforts to change the Constitution took root, and in 1912, Congress proposed an amendment to allow for direct election of senators. The Seventeenth Amendment was ratified in 1913.

BONUS FACT

Following the brawl, Gray withdrew from consideration and remained governor through the end of his term. Ultimately, a former senator named David Turpie (a Democrat) took the senate seat. But Turpie's election to the senate in 1886 only came as a result of Gray's gerrymandering, which was so aggressive that the Indiana Supreme Court later reversed the borders drawn by the governor. But don't feel too bad for the guy Turpie beat in the election; Benjamin Harrison, the Republican incumbent he bested wouldn't be out of politics for long: He was elected President of the United States in 1888.

WHEN YOU CAN'T WIN THE VOTE, WIN AT THE BAR

Redefining the Term "Liquor Closet"

When it comes to choosing elected officials, almost everything about them is up for debate; their policies, character, even physical appearance are, for better or worse, fair game. But there's one thing everyone can agree upon: Whoever wins should, in the *very* least, show up for work. You wouldn't want a legislator representing you who has a habit of failing to vote because he or she is incapacitated. This doesn't happen very often, fortunately—that is, except in the case of Edward Jerningham Wakefield.

Edward Jerningham Wakefield was born in London in June 1820 and was an early English colonist in New Zealand. Around the age of eighteen, he traveled with his father, a politician named Edwin Gibbon Wakefield who advocated for colonial expansion, to Canada on a secret mission to unite Lower and Upper Canada into one political unit. The colonization bug bit Jerningham during this trip, and shortly thereafter, he joined his uncle, Colonel William Wakefield, on an expedition to New Zealand.

Jerningham was supposed to only be in New Zealand for a few months, scouting out areas for future British colonies, but became enamored with the area. Eventually he became a permanent resident, and when New Zealand formed a parliament in 1853, he was among its first members, serving one term. He returned to private life thereafter but ultimately sought political office again in 1871. At this time he was once again elected as a member of parliament—but proved unpopular. When re-election came around four years later, he was one of six men on the ballot striving for one of just three seats. Jerningham came in fifth.

And his allies in parliament were likely very happy about this: It meant they didn't have to lock him in the closet anymore. Okay, it wasn't a closet—but close enough. You see, Jerningham had quite a drinking problem. *Te Ara* (the encyclopedia of New Zealand) details, "his later life was clouded by alcoholism and disgrace," and this alcoholism was a notable part of his second term as a member of parliament. At times, he would drink so much that he became unable to vote on legislation. Incredibly, he was not alone here—there were a few other MPs for whom the term "drop dead drunk" was only barely an exaggeration—and as a result, his sober colleagues needed to find a solution. According to *Grog's Own Country: The Story of Liquor Licensing in New Zealand*, the answer was simple: Jerningham and the other MPs in question were "locked up by Whips [legislative leaders] in small rooms to keep them sober enough to stand up for crucial [matters]." But it didn't end there.

Jerningham's political allies thought they had a foolproof plan: By keeping Jerningham behind lock and key in a room without any alcohol, they had a vote at the ready when the time came. But they made an error that only Santa Claus (and certain MPs) would have noticed: The otherwise inaccessible room that housed Jerningham had a chimney. *Grog's Own Country* explains: "On one occasion, political opponents tried to defeat the purpose of the incarceration by lowering a bottle of whisky to [Jerningham] down the chimney on a piece of string." The ploy almost worked; Jerningham drank too much initially, effectively passing out, but was able to recover in time to vote.

BONUS FACT

Is it "whisky" or "whiskey"? That depends on where the drink came from. As *Grammarist* explains, "'whisky' usually denotes Scotch whisky and Scotch-inspired liquors, and 'whiskey' denotes the Irish and American liquors."

HARRY POTTER 2.0?

The Wizard of New Zealand

As of 2018, Christchurch, New Zealand, is home to nearly 400,000 people, many of whom lead pretty normal lives with normal jobs. Ian Brackenbury Channell, though, isn't one of them. His job title: The Wizard of New Zealand.

For most of his early career, London-born Channell worked as a sociology lecturer, community organizer for adult education programs, and cultural affairs officer at universities. But his passion, it seemed, lay with the more *countercultural*. In the late 1960s, while he was a student at the University of New South Wales pursuing a PhD in sociology, Channell organized a group called "ALF" ("Action for Love and Freedom"), which hoped to usher in "The Fun Revolution." He saw this as a new path that disapproved of both the Marxism and capitalism movements of the time.

The group made Channel into a public contrarian—and it also made him unpopular with many. In 1969, he was kicked out of his PhD program for failing to do the work to progress in his studies. The vice chancellor at the University of NSW appreciated his work as a community organizer, however, and wanted to keep him on campus. Channel came up with an idea: If he couldn't be a PhD student, maybe he could be a wizard. Amazingly, the vice chancellor agreed. That year, the school had its first-ever University Wizard—a paid position funded in part by the administration and also through student union funds. The salary wasn't much, but the role gave Channel what every aspirant wants out of a first job: A foot in the door and a line on his resume.

After the 1970 school year, Channel's time as the University Wizard ended, but his career was on the right path—if you aspired to be a professional wizard, that is. In 1971, he convinced the University of Melbourne to hire him to lead a theretofore nonexistent cosmology department—a role which came with the use of a lecture hall where Channel could teach the next generation of wizards. The job, however, did not come with any pay. So, after the 1974 school year, Channel relocated to Christchurch, hoping to find new opportunities for those pursuing the magic arts.

Amazingly, he found success. Unlike Harry Potter or Gandalf the Grey, Channel wasn't capable of casting spells, but he did have a way with words. Shortly after moving to Christchurch, he began visiting the city's center, Cathedral Square, dressed in a black cloak and pointed black hat (and yes, he had a shaggy gray beard). He carried with him neither wand nor staff but rather a ladder, which he climbed to give himself a perch to speak from. The square became his classroom, and he'd give lectures to passersby on the major topics of the day or whatever else he'd care to discuss.

At first, the local authorities weren't pleased, seeing his schtick as an unwelcome disruption to the peace. The people, however, loved him, and the Christchurch City Council had no choice but to let him stay. Ultimately, they came around about the idea of having a wizard in their midst and, in 1982, made him official by naming him the first-ever Wizard of Christchurch. Eight years later, Prime Minister Mike Moore promoted him to Wizard of New Zealand, and in 2009 he was even awarded the Queen's Service Medal by the New Zealand government for his service to the nation.

BONUS FACT

Speaking of wizards, actor Sean Connery was offered the role of Gandalf in The Lord of the Rings trilogy but turned it down. Reportedly, he was unfamiliar with the novels and didn't quite understand the script. He passed up on what would turn out to be a record-setting amount of money. According to CNN, New Line Cinema offered Connery "up to 15 percent of worldwide box office receipts," which would have totaled $400 million in 2008.

FROM A CLUCK TO A CLICK

The Fowl-Powered Municipal Lighting System

Streetlights are amazing. When it's light outside, they turn off; at night, they come on. It's like magic! Actually, it's science. In most cases, the mechanism that tells a streetlight to turn on or off is a photoresistor. How they work can be complicated, but the basic idea is that when sunlight hits the resistor, the streetlamp turns off. If there is no sun, there is nothing to hit the resistor, and the light comes on.

But what about streetlights *before* photoresistors were invented? Just look to Brightwater, New Zealand, a coincidentally named town of about 1,800 people as of 2006. According to *NZ History*, the town "was named after a water-powered flour mill there." It is believed that Alfred Saunders, the owner of the mill and the man who gave the town its name, was inspired by "Bright Water," a popular song at the time that encouraged choosing nonalcoholic drinks over spirits.

Regardless of the origin, Brightwater certainly wasn't named after the hydroelectric plant that graced the town around 1910, sixty years after its founding. This hydroelectric plant was itself a repurposed flour mill—by night, at least. During the daylight hours, it still operated as a mill like any other, owned by a farmer named Robert Ellis. As the collection *No. 8 Re-Wired* details, Ellis would then use the mill to produce electricity at night. To do so, he hooked the mill up to a power grid of sorts that provided the electricity for five streetlights in town and one in the next town over. All he had to do then was trek down to the farm the next morning to disconnect the power, and the lights would turn off for the day.

But this was still a chore and one Ellis wanted to avoid if possible. So he began looking for another solution and soon found one: his chickens. Per *No. 8 Re-Wired*, Ellis "hooked up a plank to the [light] switch and put the plank in the henhouse. When the [chickens] came home each night and jumped on the plank to roost, they also turned on the lights." And the opposite happened when the chickens woke and left the henhouse: "When they went to go about their business, the plank clicked up and the power went off again."

The need for poultry-powered streetlights dissipated as technology improved. Still, Ellis's ingenuity should have made him a technological superstar in his small New Zealand town at the time, but, alas, even this wasn't meant to be. In 1908—a few years before Ellis's chickens started turning the lights on and off—a Nobel physicist named Ernest Rutherford famously developed the nucleus-centric model of the atom. It was a tough act for Ellis (or anyone else) to follow.

BONUS FACT

How much would it cost to make a chicken sandwich from scratch? That depends on what "from scratch" means and how far you want to go with it. In 2014, a *YouTuber* named Andy George decided to see what it would take if he started with almost nothing. He grew his own vegetables, ground his own wheat, harvested honey from bees, pressed his own self-grown sunflower seeds for oil, and slaughtered a chicken. The result: It was a pretty mediocre sandwich, per his own admission, at the "low" price of about $1,500.

MODERN-DAY CANARIES IN THE COAL MINES

The Chickens That Defend Disney World

In 2009, Microsoft cofounder Bill Gates gave a talk at the annual TED conference. You can watch the speech on the TED website, and while it's good, it certainly doesn't compare to the live event. That's because five minutes into his talk, Gates invited some special guests to join him in the TED auditorium: mosquitoes. The reason? Malaria. Over the years, Gates has made ending malaria a top goal (in 2018 he announced a $1 billion fund to this end), and eradication starts with mosquitoes. Mosquitoes are quite dangerous for such small creatures. By spreading disease, they claim more human lives than any other animal on earth. And they carry more than just malaria; they're also known to transmit Zika, West Nile, and Dengue fever among others.

This is precisely why Walt Disney World strategically places chickens around its theme park. Yes, chickens. Chickens, like humans, get bit by mosquitoes. If a mosquito is carrying a transmittable virus, the chicken, like any person, will end up with it too. And when the virus is significant enough, you can use a blood test to tell whether or not a chicken (or person) has been infected. But that's where the similarities between human and chickens end—at least as far as disease is concerned. As the *Los Angeles*

Times explains, chickens "never develop high enough levels of the virus in their blood to give the disease back to [uninfected] mosquitoes." This makes them effective tools in receiving early warnings about mosquito-borne diseases.

Disney World, being situated in often-muggy Florida, *should* be a hotbed for mosquitoes, and a disease outbreak at the "Happiest Place on Earth" would, of course, be a disaster. The park has done a great job of keeping the bugs away, but inevitably, mosquitoes are going to find a way in. So Disney keeps eight flocks of chicken on-site as well to mitigate any potential damage. These birds, known as "sentinel chickens," effectively operate like the proverbial canary in a coal mine. On a weekly basis, officials from Disney test the chickens' blood for antibodies of certain diseases. Hopefully, everything turns out negative, but if not, disease control officers have time to act before the illness spreads. In the very least, a positive blood test result lets park officials know that they need to redouble their efforts to eradicate mosquitoes in the area where the affected chicken was stationed.

As for the audience at Gates's TED Talk, they were fine. Gates did release the mosquitoes freely, but being bitten would cause only itchiness—not malaria (Gates made sure before he took the stage that none his mosquitoes were carrying the disease).

BONUS FACT

Greenland has mosquitoes, the United Kingdom has them, and so does Scandinavia. Yet there are no mosquitoes in Iceland. You might think it is because of cold temperatures, but remember that despite their names, Greenland is colder than Iceland. The bugs can hibernate under the ice until it's warm enough outside to mate, lay eggs, and mature those eggs. Rather, as *Iceland* magazine explains, "changes in climate in Iceland are so rapid that the mosquito does not have sufficient time to complete its lifecycle."

CHICKEN NUGGET FUEL

The Fast Food That Powers World Records

In the 1950s, a Cornell University professor named Robert C. Baker invented a product that is now well known, plentiful, and surprisingly impactful. No, it didn't cure any disease or solve any major problems, but it did play a role in extending human performance beyond previous thresholds. The product? Chicken nuggets. A look at athlete Usain Bolt explains this surprising development.

Bolt is widely regarded as the world's fastest man; as of 2018, he holds the world record in both the 100-meter and 200-meter dash. He set these records in the 2008 Olympics in Beijing and also set a world record in his other event at this time—the 4-by-100-meter relay. And he did so with flair. Take the 100-meter final, for example. As the *New Zealand Herald* noted, "not only was the record set without a favorable wind (+0.0 m/s), but he also visibly slowed down to celebrate before he finished and his shoelace was untied." Bolt won, and it wasn't close.

His successes, however, were not a function of his nutrition—or perhaps they were. After the Olympic games, Bolt hired a well-known dietician named Leslie Bonci. Before Bonci began working with Bolt, she noted that he "had horrible eating habits." Those habits included a distinct disinterest in trying the local cuisine of Beijing. In his 2013 autobiography, *Faster Than Lightning*, Bolt noted that he didn't eat much, if any, Chinese food while in Beijing, finding it "odd." Instead, he confessed to a fondness for Professor Baker's invention. As detailed in *Time* magazine, Bolt's 2008 Olympic diet was, by and large, Chicken McNuggets: "In the ten days Bolt spent in Beijing, he downed approximately 1,000 nuggets, averaging 100 a day. At 940 calories per 20-piece box, that means that Usain ate about 4,700 calories' worth of Chicken McNuggets a day and 47,000 calories over the course of his stay in China." "At first, I ate a box of 20 for lunch, then another for dinner," Usain wrote in his autobiography. "The next day I had two boxes for breakfast, one for lunch and then another couple in the evening. I even grabbed some fries and an apple pie to go with it." The end result? Three record-setting gold medals.

But please, don't try this at home—and certainly not for the purpose of becoming the next Olympic champion. In 2012, a seventeen-year-old girl in the UK ended up in the hospital with severe anemia because her diet (since age two!) had centered around at least one meal of Chicken McNuggets per day. For a healthy lifestyle, it's best to refer to the dietary recommendations of your doctor.

BONUS FACT

The world's largest chicken nugget weighed 51.1 pounds (23.2 kg). The enormous nugget was made by Empire Kosher Poultry in 2013 to promote the company's seventy-fifth anniversary (and, per the company, their improved chicken nugget recipe). The nugget was the size of approximately 750 regular-sized nuggets—or about 75 percent of the estimated number of nuggets eaten by Bolt during the 2008 Olympics.

BLOWING BROCCOLI-FLAVORED BUBBLES

Fast Food, Chewing Gum, and Vegetables— What Could Go Wrong?

In Roald Dahl's classic novel *Charlie and the Chocolate Factory*, five children are invited to a once-in-a-lifetime tour of a legendary candy factory operated by the enigmatic Willy Wonka. One of these lucky children is Violet Beauregarde, who holds the world record for the longest amount of time spent chewing one piece of gum ("over *three months solid*"). Beauregarde ultimately fails to make her way through to the end of the tour, falling prey to an experimental gum that aims to replicate the experience of a three-course dinner. When she gets to the dessert phase of the gum, her body begins transforming into a blueberry, and Violet turns, well, *violet*.

While bubble gum that replaces full meals is a work of fiction reserved for Wonka's factory, real food that mimicked the flavor of bubble gum was once very real—and as the McDonald's corporation can confirm, it wasn't a good idea. In 2014, the popular burger franchise took note of one thing Willy Wonka's chocolate factory lacked: broccoli. While this was for good reason (kids generally don't like broccoli), McDonald's decided that it was important to add healthy food choices to its menu—and if there's one thing everyone can agree upon, it's that broccoli is good for you (okay, it may make some people a bit gassy when eaten in larger quantities). While this addition to a cheeseburger Happy Meal would be great both for kids and their parents, convincing the kids to actually eat it would be another story.

To solve this anticipated problem, McDonald's borrowed an idea from the dental and pharmaceutical communities: They tried to make bubblegum-flavored broccoli. If it works for toothpaste and amoxicillin, why not broccoli too? The food scientists at the burger franchise got to work attempting to create a product that merged the nutrition of vegetables with the kid-friendly taste of artificial colors and flavors.

Not surprisingly, this experiment didn't work. The science itself was sound: Team McDonald's was able to get broccoli to taste a lot like bubble gum. But the experience of eating the product wasn't what the team had hoped for. As McDonald's then-CEO Don Thompson would explain at a gathering of venture capitalists, when testing the product it was found that kids hated the bubble gum broccoli about as much as they hated regular broccoli. According to *Business Insider*, "kids were confused by the taste"—the sweet experience didn't match what their brains anticipated.

In short, you shouldn't expect to see broccoli on the kids' menu at McDonald's any time soon. However, as the company is happy to point out, you *will* find a number of other vegetable options. As Thompson also noted, McDonald's "sells the most salads of any American restaurant chain."

BONUS FACT

Before you dive into that salad, keep in mind that not all options containing leafy greens are exactly healthy. Per McDonald's website, the Bacon Ranch Salad with Buttermilk Crispy Chicken has 490 calories and 8 grams of saturated fat per serving—only 50 calories and 2 grams of saturated fat less than a Big Mac.

BURGER MATH

The Trouble with Fractions in Ground Meat

When it comes to the innovations of burger giant McDonald's, perhaps no one deserves more praise than the late Al Bernardin. During his decades-long association with the fast-food corporation—sometimes as a corporate executive, sometimes as a franchise owner—he developed many of the items still on the menu today. He's credited with creating the Filet-O-Fish, pushing the company to add apple pies to the menu, and pioneering the switch from fresh French fries (which had to be cut on site) to frozen pre-cut ones. While most of these efforts involved help and input from his colleagues, one innovation was almost entirely his: the ever-popular Quarter Pounder.

In 1971, while running a franchise in Fremont, California, Bernardin postulated that some customers wanted more meat for their money. His idea was for a burger with a hefty beef patty—4 ounces (or 113 grams), precooked, which was more than double the size of a typical McDonald's beef patty at the time. He called the burger the "Quarter Pounder" and the next year, McDonald's corporate team added Bernardin's creation to the national menu.

It's been a trademark product of the burger chain ever since.

And it's seen some competition over the years. One competition in particular had a quite comical result, thanks to the customers. In the 1980s, A&W Restaurants wanted to be a part of this "bigger is better" burger movement. (As an aside: The restaurant chain was originally related to the root beer of the same name and still highlights the soft drink on its menu, but as of 2011 is owned by an entirely separate company.) So, they introduced a competitor to the McDonald's Quarter Pounder, offering something called the "Third Pounder." The sizable patty featured a third of a pound of beef—an obviously superior product.

Except that it wasn't so obviously superior, at least not to the customers. As *The New York Times* explained, "The A&W burger had more meat than the Quarter Pounder; in taste tests, customers preferred A&W's burger. And it was less expensive. Yet instead of leaping at the great value, customers snubbed it." Only when the company held customer focus groups did it become clear why: The Third Pounder presented the American public with a test of fractions. And the public failed. Misunderstanding the value of one third, customers believed they were being overcharged for what they perceived was less meat. Why, they asked the researchers, should they pay the same amount for a third of a pound of meat as they did for a quarter of a pound of meat at McDonald's. The "4" in "¼," being larger than the "3" in "⅓," led them astray. Not looking to solve a greater issue with math, A&W changed the name to Papa Burger.

BONUS FACT

In the 1994 movie *Pulp Fiction*, Vincent (played by John Travolta) tells Jules (Samuel L. Jackson) that in France, they don't call the "Quarter Pounder with cheese" by that name because "they've got the metric system" and therefore "they wouldn't know what the [expletive] a quarter pounder is." He explains that instead, the French call the "Quarter Pounder" the "Royale with Cheese." It makes sense—but it's incorrect; in France, a Quarter Pounder with cheese is actually called "Le Royal Cheese."

FEATHERS, LEAD, AND GOLD

When a Pound Is Not a Pound

Which weighs more, a pound of feathers or a pound of lead? When answering this age-old riddle, your instinct may be to go with the lead. After all, in equal amounts, lead *is* heavier than feathers. But it is actually a trick question: A pound is a unit of weight, so therefore, a pound of anything weighs the same as a pound of another thing.

Or does it?

If you put a pound of feathers on one side of a balance and a pound of lead on the other, the scale would rest with both sides even with one another. But what if you were to swap out the lead for gold? In that case, the balance would end up tilted, showing that the feathers weigh more. It may seem like dark magic, but it has nothing to do with the feathers or the gold: It has to do with how the weight is measured. Whenever you use the term "pound" (when discussing weight at least; it means something else when talking about cakes and British currency), you're talking about pounds as defined by something called the "avoirdupois system." It's the standard, non-metric system you're familiar with if you live in the United States.

In the avoirdupois system, there are 16 ounces in 1 pound. One avoirdupois ounce is equal to about 28.35 grams. Multiply those 16 ounces per pound by 28.35 grams, and you end up with about 453.6 grams per avoirdupois pound.

Feathers are measured in avoirdupois pounds, and so is just about everything else—from cheese and rubber bands to graphite and, yes, lead. But gold is a special case. It, and other precious metals and gemstones, are measured in something called "troy pounds." (It's unclear why that is, as the origin of the troy weight system has been lost over the course of history.) A troy pound is equal to about 12 ounces, and a troy ounce is equal to about 31.1 grams. Multiply the 12 ounces by 31.1 grams, and it comes to about 373.2 grams per troy pound—or about 20 percent less than what a pound of feathers weighs.

So if you want to win a bar bet, put a pound of feathers on one side of your (hypothetical) balance, and a troy pound of gold on the other side. The feathers will weigh more. Of course, testing this in real life may be a little tougher to manage; first, you'd need a balance that can accommodate roughly 50,000 feathers. Second, you'd need to make quite the ATM withdrawal, as a troy pound of gold costs more than $10,000 as of 2018. However, if you did manage to overcome these hurdles, you'd come away victorious.

BONUS FACT

You probably have a little bit of gold in your pocket right now! Gold is very conductive and doesn't corrode or oxidize easily, making it very useful for small, portable electronic devices. So, if you have an iPhone or Android device on hand, you're golden. Each of these devices has about 0.001 troy ounces of gold in it—worth approximately $1.50 as of 2019.

DON'T TRY THIS AT HOME...
OR ANYWHERE ELSE

The App That Aims to Break Your Smartphone

If you own a smartphone, such as an iPhone or Android, you have something called an accelerometer. The accelerometer is basically a high-tech gyroscope: It detects your phone's movements up and down, left and right, and side to side. While this may seem like insignificant information, being able to measure such movements has a lot of practical value. It allows games to be more immersive, virtual and augmented reality experiences to be achievable, navigation systems to measure your speed, and much more. It also has a lot of less-than-practical uses. For example, if you threw your smartphone up in the air as high as you could, the accelerometer would measure roughly about how high you threw it. Okay, so maybe that's a bad example. After all, no one would do that, right? Wrong.

In the summer of 2013, a Norwegian developer firm named CarrotPop came out with a new app called S.M.T.H., or "Send Me to Heaven." It is a game—a dare, really—in which players would bravely (or perhaps foolishly?) throw their devices skyward in the hopes of winning...well, nothing, unless you included the pride of being at the top of the in-app leaderboard. The higher your phone flew, the higher your name went on this board; the only caveat was the anti-cheating algorithms that aimed to detect descents that were too slow (i.e., when a phone was aided by a parachute or something similar).

A bit crazy? Yes. But people enjoyed playing. *Time* magazine reported on the lengths some people went to achieve great heights: "[As of August 2013], the top score is held by someone who threw a phone more than 40 meters (about 131 feet) high, which the app's designer Petr Svarovsky attributes to people building slingshots to catapult their phones and posting photos of them on *Facebook*."

If you want to try the game for yourself, you can—as long as you have an Android phone. The app is available for free in the Google Play store, with more than 7,000 reviews averaging 4 stars as of 2019. But phone-tossers beware; as one review in the Play Store notes, it can be risky: "It was really fun until I accidentally threw it on the concrete up 4.3 meters and my screen cracked really badly. It's $90 to repair. If you're going to download this do it on a phone you don't care about."

If you are an iPhone user interested in playing the game, however, you're out of luck. Per *Wired*, Apple "determined the game was 'encouraging behavior that would result in damage to the user's device'" and banned it from its app store. Svarovsky wasn't happy with the ban, but don't feel bad just yet; the ban didn't undercut his business, but rather, his ultimate goal. As Svarovsky told *Wired*, he was no fan of these phones, believing that "people in certain societies buy [them] just to show off." *Wired* explained that he "hoped to have people shatter as many iPhones as possible." For better or for worse, it is unclear how successful Svarovsky was in this plan; the S.M.T.H. leaderboard may measure heights achieved, but not smartphone casualties.

BONUS FACT

In many contexts (classrooms, religious ceremonies, and courts) it's a good idea to make sure your phone is off or silenced. That is especially true in the courtroom of Judge Hugh Clarke. In May 2013, he instituted a policy where, if your phone rang, he'd cite you for contempt of court and confiscate the device until you paid a $50 fine. In October of that year, he even got to use the policy twice in one hearing. First the defendant's phone rang. Then, a few minutes later, another phone rang: Judge Clarke's. Not wanting to be a hypocrite, he held himself in contempt, handing $50 to the court officer.

THE PRIZE IS IN THE DETAILS

Why It Pays to Read the Fine Print

If you've ever downloaded an app via iTunes, Apple has prompted you to first agree to its End User License Agreement, or EULA. Unless you are an interested attorney or have strange hobbies, you likely click through this agreement without actually reading it. And there's good reason for that. Here is a small taste of what you'd see if you were intent on muddling your way through it: "This license granted to You for the Licensed Application by Application Provider is limited to a nontransferable license to use the Licensed Application on any iPhone or iPod touch that You own or control and as permitted by the Usage Rules set forth in Section 9.b. of the App Store Terms and Conditions (the "Usage Rules"). This license does not allow You to use the Licensed Application on any iPod touch or iPhone that You do not own or control, and You may not distribute or make the Licensed Application available over a network where it could be used by multiple devices at the same time."

Yawn. And that was only two sentences! It is not just boring, but confusing. For most, figuring out what is said in a company's EULA and what it even means is incredibly difficult if not outright impossible. Regardless, you want to use the service, so agreeing to these terms is necessary no matter what you might think about them. The payoff for fully reading this long text is zero. Except when there's a reward hidden inside, that is.

In the early 2000s, a small software company called PC Pitstop wanted to see just how often EULAs were ignored yet agreed to by consumers. As their test, they added a special section in their own EULA that read: "A special consideration which may include financial compensation will be awarded to a limited number of authorized licensees to read this section of the license agreement and contact PC Pitstop at consideration@pcpitstop.com. This offer can be withdrawn at any time." The "financial compensation" turned out to be a check for $1,000.

The agreement now released to the public, they waited. And waited. In fact, they waited for four months before someone finally emailed the consideration@pcpitstop.com address. In those four months, roughly 3,000 people installed PC Pitstop's software—clearly without closely reading the agreement. When one man, named Doug Heckman, finally did, he learned that the $30 piece of software he purchased was a winning lottery ticket. Reading the fine print actually paid off.

The $1,000 prize was more than just a social experiment for PC Pitstop, however. It was also the center of a PR and marketing campaign designed to bring attention to one of their products: anti-spyware software. As the company explained in an email newsletter to its customers, "spyware and adware love to hide their bad news in the EULA, and after our experiment we can understand why." Beyond opening consumer eyes to the importance of reading the fine print, they positioned their software as a key part of catching these kinds of hacks and keeping computers safe.

BONUS FACT

More evidence that people don't read the iTunes EULA? You probably didn't notice that it says that "You also agree that you will not use these products for any purposes prohibited by United States law, including, without limitation, the development, design, manufacture, or production of nuclear, missile, or chemical or biological weapons." So please, do not create weapons of mass destruction via iTunes. After all, you wouldn't want to lose access to your playlists on your quest for world domination.

DO NOT SKIP THIS UNDER PENALTY OF LAW

Why Mattresses Come with Warning Tags

If you live in the United States and have ever looked at your bed mattress while changing the sheets, you have likely noticed an interesting tag. In ominous terms, this tag warns you not to remove it. If you do, FBI agents will appear, cascading down from a helicopter, crashing through your bedroom windows, and carting you off to a prison on some distant island not even known to most mapmakers.

No, not really. The tag does state that it is illegal to remove it, but it isn't a warning meant for consumers. As the consumer at least, you can remove the tag without repercussion. But that hasn't stopped it from becoming the subject of countless jokes. Most notably the tag has been lampooned by Dilbert, Pee-wee Herman, and *National Lampoon* magazine. There's even a commercial by Serta (a mattress company) in which the removal of one of the tags results in the culprits—sheep—being put in jail. In fairness, sheep are not exactly part of the consumer market most mattress companies have in mind.

So, with a warning that seems ridiculous to so many, why is

the tag there in the first place? The answer involves looking back at earlier versions of the mattress you dread leaving every morning. Today, there's not a lot of reason to think that the contents of your mattress are anything other than what you bargained for—but that wasn't always the case. Before springs and coils and memory foam, mattresses were filled with straw and other cheap, safe materials. Unfortunately, there were a lot of less-than-honest vendors out there. *Mental Floss* explains: "[In the early 20th century], mattresses were often constructed with some unsavory stuffing—horse hair, corn husks, food waste, old rags, newspaper, and whatever else a manufacturer could come by were regularly shoved inside. Consumers would never see the stuffing, so no harm, no foul, right? Not really. Some of this stuff harbored bacteria and household pests that gave unwary consumers a not-so-restful slumber."

The tag was thus designed to hold manufacturers accountable for disclosing what was in the mattress. Law required them to print what was inside on the outside of the mattress. Manufacturers could still lie, but doing so would mean risking being discovered later on; a government inspector could obtain one of the mattresses for an impromptu check, and if anything other than what was listed was inside, the manufacturer would be subject to fines and other penalties.

There remained a problem, however: You could still comply with that law when stuffing a mattress with anything. And that's what a lot of manufacturers did; they carried on using rags, newspapers, animal hair, and more. No one was going to buy these mattresses, of course, but the industry had a way around that too. The inspectors would do their spot checks while the mattresses were still in the manufacturers' care, then once that was over, the manufacturers or retailers would simply remove the labels. Consumers were no better off than they were before.

To put an end to this issue, Congress made it illegal to re-move the tag "prior to the time any textile fiber product is sold and delivered to the ultimate consumer." And, perhaps to protect themselves, manufacturers also printed a "do not remove" warning on the tag itself. So, if you want to remove the one tag from your mattress, rest assured that you can do so with impunity. Just make sure the tag doesn't claim that the mattress is stuffed with old corn husks—or worse—first!

BONUS FACT

If you live in Norway and own a cow, you better get that cow a mattress. Per a 2009 NPR report, "new rules went into effect in Norway aimed at easing the life of cows, who really like to lounge." This means each cow owned has to be given a mattress to lie on. The cow mattress is just foam with a rubber top—nothing fancy—but it gets the job done. Apparently, it's good for the dairy farmer too. NPR explains, "it turns out that comfy cows give about 5 percent more milk."

CHILDREN OF THE BOX

The Finnish Approach to Raising Babies

Babies typically sleep in cribs, but if you're a parent who can't afford one, it can be a problem for the young child's health and well-being. In the mid-1930s, infant death rates in Finland were a very high 65 out of 1,000 live births. Social scientists attributed many of these deaths to two factors. First, expectant parents sought too little prenatal care (often because they were unable to afford it). Second, they brought the baby into a house with inadequate materials: too few diapers, not enough clothes, and often nowhere to sleep. And as any parent of a newborn will tell you, the worst time to figure out what you need for a baby is when you come home after giving birth.

To solve this problem, Finland came up with a creative idea: A gift box, delivered to your home before your due date. Early gift boxes contained diapers, bedsheets, socks, and the like, as well as extra fabric so expectant mothers could create clothes for their newborns. Over the years, the boxes would grow into quite the cornucopias, with modern boxes each containing a little mattress and bedding; a snowsuit set with mittens, a hat, and booties; bodysuits, socks, and other everyday wear; bathroom items, such as a towel and toothbrush; and even bra pads and condoms. The aim was to deliver all of the things you'd need for your little one (and some other items for your own care).

All the would-be mother needed to do to receive a baby gift box was seek out a doctor for a few checkups during the pregnancy. The gift box program, which was originally provided only to low-income families, soon became very popular, and now is a staple of Finnish culture. All expectant mothers who seek prenatal care are offered a box, and almost all of them (approximately 95 percent) take it. The remaining 5 percent take a small cash amount instead.

The most distinctive part of the gift box offering—and the item that best defines the Finnish newborn culture—is the box itself. Because many of the poorest households in the 1930s couldn't afford cribs, the boxes were specifically designed to act as a basic crib. According to the BBC, a majority of today's Finnish community grows up—for a few weeks or months, at least—sleeping in a baby box. And the boxes proved to be instrumental in helping the original problem of high infant mortality. The rate fell from a peak nearing 90 per 1,000 in the 1940s to the single digits by the late 1970s. As of 2019, Finland has one of the lowest infant mortality rates in the world.

BONUS FACT

You probably don't think of Finland as a third world nation, but under the original definition of the term, it was. The term was coined during the Cold War. The "first world" countries were the United States and other NATO-aligned nations, while the "second world" included the Soviet Union, China, and its allies. Unaligned nations—including Finland—were given the "third world" moniker. The economies of most of the other original "third world" countries were still developing at the time, hence the misconception that "third world" is related to the strength of a nation's economy.

LIFTING THE OLD BALL AND CHAIN

Couples That Literally Carry Their Relationships on Their Backs

Taisto Miettinen and Kristiina Haapalainen aren't household names, but perhaps they should be. The duo are world champions many times over, beating out the competition from 2009 to 2013 in their sport of choice. You won't see them at the Olympics, however, because the sport Miettinen and Haapalainen dominated isn't one that awards gold medals. No, the winning couple in this sport receives the female team member's weight in beer. Welcome to the Wife Carrying World Championships!

While the origins of this competition aren't cemented in record, it is believed that it comes from an apocryphal story from Finland's history. Legend has it that in the mid-nineteenth century, a gang leader named Herkko Rosvo-Ronkainen devised a test for potential gang members. To prove their worth, they had to carry either a sack of grains (per some accounts) or a live pig (per other accounts) over sandy pits, through ponds, and around various other obstacles. In addition, Rosvo-Ronkainen's men were known to steal young women from nearby villages, likely as a way of picking wives.

In 1992, the small Finnish municipality of Sonkajärvi decided to combine these legendary "traditions" into an annual athletic event. Men would participate in an obstacle course similar to what Rosvo-Ronkainen's recruits had to go through, but instead of carrying sacks of grain or squealing pigs, they were to carry their wives. Every year since, typically in August, couples from around the world (though primarily from Northern Europe) have gathered in Sonkajärvi to try and tackle the 253.5-meter track.

The rules of the competition are fairly simple. Men are permitted to wear a lifting belt and women are allowed to wear a helmet, but no other safety or performance-enhancing equipment is allowed. Any type of carry is allowed, but the most common ones are the traditional "fireman's carry," where the husband carries the wife over his shoulder, and the "Estonian-style" carry, where the woman wraps her legs around the man's shoulders and hangs upside down with her arms around his waist. The woman has to weigh at least 49 kg (108 pounds), and if she's underweight, she has to carry a rucksack heavy enough to get her to that 49 kg minimum. The competition is broken down into races between two couples, and while you're trying to beat the other couple to the finish line, you are also racing against the clock. Once every couple has gone and the winners from each race are singled out, the couple that took the least amount of time to get over the finish line wins the beer.

What if you're an unmarried man (or if your wife doesn't like the idea of being carried upside down through water hazards and sand traps) but want to compete? Don't worry: You still can! The word "wife" in "Wife Carrying World Championship" is flexible; as the official rules state, "the wife to be carried may be your own, or the neighbor's, or you may have found her farther afield; she must, however, be over 17 years of age."

BONUS FACT

Wife carrying isn't the only weird sport out there. Among the many odd competitions you can find out there is one called "bog snorkeling." Participants don flippers and snorkels and navigate their way through a trench dug out of a peat bog. And it has something in common with the wife carrying competition: Taisto Miettinen is a world champion in both.

THE SIEGE OF WEINSBERG

The Women Who Shouldered the Load for Their Families

Throughout the Middle Ages, the European continent was fraught with violence and unrest. Every time a leader passed away, a power struggle would ensue. Compassion for the defeated party was rarely seen; when warring factions clashed, the victors would often kill the men who had been loyal to the defeated lord. The lives of their wives and children would fortunately be spared, but the victors would often claim the family as their own.

The events following the death of German King (and Holy Roman Emperor) Lothair II in 1137 would begin in a similar way, but would ultimately prove quite unique. When Lothair died, there wasn't a clear heir to take his place, and two different houses had their eye on the now-empty throne. He himself had claimed membership to the House of Welf throughout his reign, but only as a matter of political convenience. Before becoming king he married off one of his children, a daughter named Gertrude, to Henry X, the Duke of Bavaria. Henry was a member of the House of Welf and this marriage gave Lothair that house's support as he sought the throne. However, Gertrude and Henry's son, known as Henry the Lion, did not become king upon Lothair's death. Instead, the House of Hohenstaufen, a competing dynastic family, secured power. Under the leadership of King Conrad III, the Hohenstaufen began to push the Welfs out of the region, and as a result, Henry the Lion declared war on the competing house.

As part of the ensuing war, Conrad's forces came to the German city of Weinsberg. In this city stood a castle garrisoned by those loyal to the Welfs, and the Hohenstaufens attacked, intending to leave it in ruin, killing the men and imprisoning the women and children. However, the defenders of Weinsberg capitulated, as its women agreed to surrender—though not quite unconditionally. Their terms? The Hohenstaufens would allow the Welf women to leave freely, and not empty-handed, either; the women would be allowed to keep whatever they could carry on their shoulders. King Conrad III agreed, but he wasn't exactly expecting what came next. Leaving material possessions behind, the women came out of the castle with their husbands slung across their backs. Conrad, believing that a king should hold true to his word, allowed the women (and their husbands) to leave in peace before raiding the now-empty castle.

Like most stories from the Middle Ages, there is a good chance that this tale has been shaped and retold in different ways over time. However there is still good reason to believe that it is true. The first known record of the events at Weinsberg comes from a source called *Chronica regia Coloniensis*, which was written only thirty-five years after the siege occurred. Further, the name of the ruins themselves offers a glimpse into the history of the battle: They are named "Weibertreu," which translates into English as "wifely loyalty."

Many castles have a moat around the outside, and typically, moats are thought of as being filled with water to keep invaders away. But what if there's a better way? In 1707, the lords of Český Krumlov Castle in what is now the Czech Republic created a different kind of moat—one filled with live bears. While it's unknown if the bears were ever called into action to protect the castle, they certainly found a home, and many generations of bears have lived there for the hundreds of years since their ancestors first arrived. Today, the moat is a zoo.

UNLIKELY ALLIES

When the Germans and Americans Teamed Up in World War II

Even if you don't know much about World War II, you probably know that the United States and Germany were on opposing sides. And for the most part, you're right. Still, a look at the waning days of the war prove that even this assumption is, at least in one instance in Austria, incorrect.

If you travel to Austria today, you may visit a small castle dating back to approximately 1240. This structure, known as Castle Itter, is just south of the German border. After Germany annexed Austria prior to the beginning of the war, the Nazi regime leased the castle from its owner, and in 1943 they seized it outright. Shortly thereafter, the German military converted the castle into a prison for about a dozen high-profile French prisoners, including Charles de Gaulle's sister, two former French military leaders, and two former French prime ministers.

The prisoners' freedom seemed likely when, on April 30, 1945, Adolf Hitler took his own life. Four days later, the commanding officer of the castle fled and his soldiers followed shortly behind. Despite the soldiers being gone, the prisoners knew that they were hardly free; the area was still under German military control, and many other fleeing soldiers would still seek shelter at the castle. Instead of making a run for it, the prisoners collected the arms that were left behind and resolved to defend themselves when the SS troops returned to retake the castle. The hope was that a liberation force would arrive in time to rescue them. In order to increase those odds, a Yugoslavian prisoner named Zvonimir Čučković—an electrician reassigned from Dachau to assist in the castle's repairs—risked recapture (or death) and set out beyond the castle's walls to find help.

What he found during his trip away from the castle were two things: Germans and Americans. The latter was welcome—but surprisingly so was the former. German commander Major Josef Gangl had already been convinced that his country was going to lose—during the weeks before Hitler's suicide, Gangl and his troops were already assisting the Austrian resistance against Hitler's forces. So, when the Castle Itter prisoner found Gangl, Gangl decided to move his unit to the castle, with the express intent of freeing the prisoners by surrendering to the Americans. Along the way back, Čučković and Gangl's group met up with a small American tank unit led by Lieutenant Jack Lee, whom they welcomed into the castle with them. The castle was now under American control.

On May 5, 1945, however, Gangl's country mates made it clear that the major did not speak for his nation. An SS unit opened fire on the castle, first with machine guns and later with anti-tank weaponry. The joint US-German forces (with support from the French captives) struggled to hold the castle, and, as *HistoryNet* notes, the Nazi loyalists seemed poised for victory. As a last-ditch effort, French tennis star Jean Borotra, one of the former prisoners, volunteered to run to a nearby village in hopes of directing reinforcements. Borotra's run was successful; American reinforcements arrived just before the Nazis made their assault on the castle's front gate. The SS troops fled, and the Americans—assisted by German soldiers for the first and only time in World War II—won the Battle for Castle Itter.

BONUS FACT

Many medieval castles feature spiral staircases that, from the point of view of someone going up the stairs, run clockwise. Why? The design makes things difficult for would-be attackers. Assuming the attackers are right-handed (as most people are), they'd be at a distinct disadvantage; as they came up the stairs, their swords would be positioned on the inside of the staircase and, therefore, would be blocked by the central pillar. Meanwhile, those defending the castle would have their swords unencumbered as they came down the stairs.

SPUDS AWAY!

*How Potatoes Impacted a
World War II Naval Battle*

The USS *O'Bannon* was a warship that served in the United States Navy during both World War II and the Korean War. The destroyer's armament was impressive by any measure: depth charges for submarines, seventeen anti-aircraft guns, torpedo tubes for ships and subs alike, and five 5"/38 caliber guns for surface targets. There were few threats that the *O'Bannon* (and other ships in its class) didn't have an answer for.

In April 1943, while in the Pacific, the *O'Bannon*'s crew was faced with one such exception. The warship detected the *Ro-34*, a Japanese submarine, which for some reason had surfaced. The *O'Bannon*'s officers decided to ram the *Ro-34*, an action that would have almost certainly sunk the sub while doing little damage to the destroyer. However, before the *O'Bannon* made contact, its leadership realized that their plan had one major flaw: The *Ro-34*, the officers feared, may have been laying mines in the water (a reasonable conclusion given that it had come to the surface), and therefore, getting the *O'Bannon* too close could be prove fatal. The *O'Bannon* turned sharply, avoiding its intended collision, and ended up cruising right next to the submarine (which, it turned out, wasn't laying mines).

As it turned out, the Japanese crew had the Americans exactly where they wanted them. The *O'Bannon* had no way of defending itself in this instance, as none of its impressive weapons were designed for close combat. Those 5"/38 caliber guns, for example, could hit targets ten or twenty football fields away, sure, but ten or twenty meters? Not a chance. To make matters worse, the crewmen aboard the *O'Bannon* weren't expected to be in close combat, so they weren't carrying handguns. Even though they could have shot the Japanese submariners pretty easily, they simply weren't armed to do so. The Japanese officers turned to their surface gun, intending to fire on the *O'Bannon*.

At a loss for what to do next, the sailors looked around for any available projectile to hurl at their enemies. And there was a plentiful one nearby: potatoes. In most cases, throwing potatoes wouldn't be a very good plan. While airborne tubers can hurt, they're no match for a submarine-mounted gun. Yet, by some stroke of luck, the large number of flying potatoes were unexpectedly effective. The Japanese crew didn't think they were being bombarded with starchy vegetables; rather, they thought the Americans were throwing hand grenades. Fearing the onslaught of hand-thrown explosives, the Japanese took cover, leaving the gun on the deck unmanned as the ship retreated from the *O'Bannon* and began its descent beneath the surface. This was, to say the least, a mistake. Had the Japanese officers simply ignored the flying potatoes (or stored them for eating later), the submarine would have likely inflicted heavy damage to the destroyer. By fleeing, they not only gave up the upper hand but also put themselves in harm's way; the *O'Bannon* now had enough distance between itself and the *Ro-34* to fire its weapons and launch it depth charges—which it did with great success. With help from another US destroyer, the *O'Bannon* sank the *Ro-34*.

BONUS FACT

In the late 1700s, there was a very successful British racehorse named Potoooooooo (pronounced "potatoes"). The reason for the strange spelling? The horse's name was originally spelled "Pot-8-Os," but a stable boy got confused and wrote out eight "o"s on the horse's feed bin. The horse's owner, amused by the alternative spelling, kept it.

THE WHITE GLOVE TREATMENT

When The Beatles Changed Fashion Overseas

Picture a police officer in your head. Chances are, the person you're visualizing is wearing a navy blue uniform. Across countries and cultures, this is typically (of course, not always) the case. The reason for these uniforms being blue is believed to be a simple matter of timing combined with the inertia of history. In the United States, police uniforms came en vogue starting in the mid- to late 1850s. When the Civil War ended, the surplus Union uniforms—which were blue—were repurposed by municipal police forces. Over time, blue shirts, blue pants, and even blue ties and blue hats became the norm for police officers across the country.

But not gloves. By and large, police officers only wear gloves if weather or other factors (e.g., if they're riding a motorcycle) dictate they do so. Unless they're in Japan, that is. It's quite common for Japanese officers to wear white gloves, actually—and the Beatles deserve some of the credit for this.

In February 1964, The Beatles made their way from England to the United States for the first time. Every step of the way, the Fab Four were besieged by fans. When they arrived at Heathrow

Airport in London for their flight across the Atlantic, an estimated 4,000 fans were there to send them off; a similar number was waiting for their arrival at John F. Kennedy Airport in New York later that day. Crowds camped out near Manhattan's Plaza Hotel when the band was staying there, and when The Beatles arrived back in the UK in late February, as many as 10,000 fans were there to greet them. And where there are crowds, there are police officers there to help ensure that everything remains relatively peaceful and safe. And by and large, they were successful in keeping this peace during The Beatles' tour.

When the Beatles returned to the US in August that year, and then again in August 1965, the situation was mostly the same: lots of fans, lots of police, and thankfully, not too many injuries. So when The Beatles announced a tour of Germany, Japan, and the Philippines for the early summer of 1966, law enforcement in each of these three areas already had a blueprint for how to best deal with the crowds. Japan, however, went a step further.

According to *The Japan Times*, the officer in charge of security for the trip, Hideo Yamada, wanted to ensure that the officers remembered that the fans weren't criminals, just young, energetic, and eager to get a glimpse of their pop idols. The police were there to keep the peace, not start a fight, and Yamada wanted to put his officers in the right mindset. Specifically, Yamada wanted them to emulate the Imperial Guard—a subsidiary organization of Japan's National Police Agency whose officers were held to a higher standard of conduct. The Imperial Guard was expected to practice an extraordinary degree of "reigi tadashisa," which translates to "propriety" or "politeness." Yamada figured that if he wanted his officers to mirror the guard's behavior, he should have them also mirror their attire. He recalled that the Imperial Guard officers wore white gloves and insisted that his officers do the same.

Whether Yamada's plan worked is unknown; there were very

few reports of unrest during The Beatles' visit to Japan (which is a promising sign). The best evidence that they were effective? White gloves became a mainstay of Japanese police uniforms from that point on.

BONUS FACT

It's not uncommon for members of the UK's royal family to wear gloves, though a gloveless royal would hardly be newsworthy— usually. In 1987, Princess Diana's small act of not wearing gloves made international news. She was at London's Middlesex Hospital for the opening of the nation's first unit built specifically to treat those with HIV/AIDS. At the time, the stigma around the disease was extraordinarily high, and many believed that any sort of physical contact with someone affected could transmit the disease. To demonstrate this wasn't true, Diana shook bare hands with one of the patients.

A SMOKE BREAK FOR NONSMOKERS

*The Smoking Cessation Program
That Works by Not Working*

There are a lot of reasons to avoid smoking cigarettes, major ones being that they're highly addictive and smoking too many can lead to a number of diseases (which is a really bad combination). But here's one reason that probably doesn't make your list: Smoking may cost you vacation time.

Per a number of studies, smokers tend to feel the pangs of withdrawal—that craving for another cigarette—sometimes just four hours after finishing one. For your typical 9-to-5 employee, that can be a problem, as it all but necessitates breaks during the workday. All told, it's not uncommon for smokers to spend an average of ten minutes per break, multiple times per day, having a cigarette to keep the jitters away. That's a drain on worker productivity, for sure, but it's one that most companies overlook.

Not Piala, a marketing firm in Japan, however. In 2017, an anonymous employee at Piala made the point via the company's suggestion box that while smokers could slack on the job for a few minutes each day, nonsmokers were given no such leeway. This was simply unfair: Everyone, smokers and nonsmokers alike, arrived at work at the same time and left at the same time. Why should the smoking group get to take breaks while the nonsmoking group had to be at their desks at all times?

While some companies may have simply issued some placating remarks in response to the complaint, Piala's leadership decided to come up with an officewide policy instead. They realized, however, that cracking down on smoking would be difficult. According to *The New York Times*, approximately one third of its employees smoked at the time, and having them all go into nicotine fits wouldn't be productive *or* safe. So they came up with another idea: compensatory time off. Ten to fifteen minutes each day, five days a week, for fifty-two weeks each year comes to about forty-eight hours per year. Assuming an eight-hour workday, that's six days' worth of work that smokers are not actually working. Piala decided to level the playing field. In response to the anonymous complaint, the company changed its vacation policy; from that point forward, nonsmokers were given six extra days of paid time off to make up for the difference.

In fairness to the smokers, the policy's purpose wasn't to admonish them for their breaks—certainly, employees of all stripes find ways to waste time during the day (for example texting friends or playing games on one's phone). The company's CEO, Takao Asuka, told the press about his true motive: "I hope to encourage employees to quit smoking through incentives rather than penalties or coercion." And it may have worked! According to CNBC, shortly after the policy was announced, four of the forty-two smokers at the company tried to kick the habit.

BONUS FACT

As of December 1, 2012, all cigarette brands offered for sale in Australia have to be sold in plain packaging in the government-mandated color, Pantone 448 C. Originally described as a drab, olive green color, Pantone 448 C was chosen because of market research suggesting that it was the ugliest option. While most were pleased with the efforts to make smoking as unattractive as possible, not everyone liked how the color was spoken about. Specifically, the Australian Olive Association objected; they didn't want olives associated with either smoking or ugly colors. As a result, Pantone 448 C is now typically described as a "drab dark brown."

AT LEAST THEY'RE HIGH IN K

Bananas and the Psychedelic Experience

In the mid-1960s, a new generation of Americans took a vocal approach to the issues of the day: anti-war sit-ins, free speech protests, civil rights marches—the list goes on. This antiestablishment movement became known collectively as the counterculture phenomenon, in which participants dispensed with many norms and embraced taboos that older generations had avoided. One major taboo was the use of illegal drugs. In fact, recreational drug use—marijuana and LSD in particular—became a hallmark of the movement. The powers that be attempted to curtail these activities, and a nationwide drug debate raged on through the late 1960s and into the 1970s. In October 1970, Congress passed the Comprehensive Drug Abuse Prevention and Control Act, and the next year, President Richard Nixon called drug use "public enemy number one."

But before the government took action, the drug world went bananas—literally. In March 1967, the *Berkeley Barb*, an underground newspaper that was well respected and well read in counterculture circles, published a story about a new way to get high: smoking banana peels. According to the *Barb*, bananas contained stimulants that, if taken correctly and in high enough amounts, could give you a psychedelic experience similar to taking LSD. Per the *Barb*, all one had to do was "freeze the peels, break and reduce to a pulp in a blender, put in the oven (low heat, 200 degrees [Fahrenheit]) until it's dry enough to smoke," and then start puffing.

Skeptical? You have every reason to be: The report was a lie. The *Barb*'s editor and publisher, Max Scherr, was trying to make a point. Authorities had been reflexively taking action against anyone and anything related to drugs, and Scherr thought they may believe his report and ban bananas. After all, he reasoned, one can't have a young, impressionable teenager walking into the local grocery store and leaving with a cheap, potassium-filled snack that, as it turns out, could get him or her high. If LSD was illegal, shouldn't the equally potent banana be as well?

The police didn't take the bait—but others did. Many people who wanted to get high took the *Barb* at its word, and from spring to summer of that year, smoking banana peels was all the rage. Banana peel smoke-ins became common among the "make love, not war" crowd. Some more entrepreneurial types even began selling dried banana powder and similar products made of processed banana peels. The so-called "active ingredient" in banana peels even got a name of its own: "bananadine." Around the country, members of the countercultural movement were reporting the same: If you wanted a cheap, easy high, smoke up some banana peels.

Ultimately, the Food and Drug Administration investigated the claims and found that there was nothing hallucinogenic in banana peels, smoked or otherwise. Any claims to the contrary were likely the placebo effect in action.

BONUS FACT

Interstate 70 runs from Maryland to Utah, crossing through Colorado along the way. Mile marker 420 *should* be seen on the interstate as one drives through Colorado, but it's not there. That's because of frequent theft—almost certainly due to the number's association with marijuana. In response to these repeated thefts, the Colorado Department of Transportation eventually developed a new mile marker sign; it reads "419.99."

URINE TROUBLE

Can You Sell Your Own Pee?

You don't think much of it—if anything. A few times a day; a few minutes per each interruption in your daily life. And yet, everyone does it—and without a choice in the matter. Yes, everyone pees.

Sometimes, this also means using a plastic cup. For most, leaving a urine sample for the doctor is part of an annual physical. And while you may not think much of this either, that sample can help your doctor understand a lot about what's going on in your body. A urine test can detect kidney disease, diabetes, and pregnancy. It's also the most common way to see whether someone is using illicit drugs. For someone who uses illegal drugs, therefore, leaving a urine sample is a problem: It's almost certainly going to paint a picture of guilt. There are some urine-masking agents out there, but their effectiveness is questionable. Your only real bet is to give a clean sample. And the easiest way to do that is to simply not use drugs. Or you could *buy* some drug-free urine—maybe.

In the mid-1990s, a South Carolina man named Kenneth Curtis was working as a pipefitter, an occupation that required him to undergo a drug test every time he started working at a new construction site. He told *Wired* magazine that he found this requirement "humiliating and degrading," and so "he donated his urine to nervous buddies as a form of protest." It turned out that other workers were interested in some of Curtis's drug-free urine as well. And some were even offering to pay a fee for it.

Curtis saw an opportunity, and in 1996, he started a rather unique business. For $69 per kit, a customer would get a pouch of drug-free urine (and no need to take Curtis's word for it: Each sample was lab-certified), a tube to help the buyer transport the liquid from the pouch to a sample cup, and a warming packet to make sure the tester didn't wonder why that urine sample wasn't warm like a fresh-from-the-body sample should be. His business boomed, and before long, Curtis had made this endeavor his full-time job. He began drinking a lot of coffee, fruit juice, and tea, and let nature's call guide most of the rest of his day. At his peak, Curtis was producing enough urine to fulfill fifty orders per day, stocking the excess—at one point 500 gallons—in industrial freezers.

Unfortunately, customers weren't the only ones who noticed Curtis's product. The South Carolinian government did as well—and many legislators weren't happy about it. In 1999, the state passed a law that made it illegal to "sell, give away, distribute, or market urine…with the intent of using the urine to defraud a drug or alcohol screening test." The police came for Curtis shortly thereafter; in April of 2001 he was caught through a sting operation when he sold a few ounces of drug-free pee to an undercover police officer at a gas station. He was convicted under the new law, sentenced to six months in prison, ordered to pay a fine of $10,000, and put on probation for five years after his prison sentence ended.

Curtis appealed the sentence and lost, although it's unclear if he ever served his jail time. He didn't give up on his business, though. Per his website, PrivacyPro.com, he continues to offer the same product, minus the urine, "to continue to service and protect...customers from invasive testing and continue the fight against the urine testing industry." The pee-free version costs $49—although it's unclear if anyone was still interested in buying the product without its original key ingredient.

BONUS FACT

During the Vietnam War, many American servicemen fell prey to heroin addiction: It was readily available and provided an escape from the horrors of war. In response, the Nixon administration refused to let servicemen in Vietnam back into the US until they passed a drug test. While they could try to detox, CNN's Dr. Sanjay Gupta noted that "expectations were low, given the extraordinary addictiveness of heroin." Studies vary, but heroin relapse rates can be as high as 90 percent. But Nixon's detox plan, informally known as "Operation Golden Flow," worked. Only about 5 percent of those who went through the detox relapsed.

YOU DON'T KNOW WHAT YOU'RE SWIMMING IN

Yes, They Can Tell If You Pee in the Pool

"We don't swim in your toilet, so please don't pee in our pool," reads the sign at many community pools. It's a good rule, although, let's face it, it's also a frequently ignored one. All too often (and really, once is too often), someone decides to take the lazy route to alleviate themselves, and simply goes in the water. It's virtually undetectable, though; as rumor-debunking website *Snopes* attests, "No matter what your parents might have told you, there isn't any magical chemical that when added to a swimming pool will reveal the presence of urine in the water by producing a brightly colored cloud."

So, okay, maybe they can't tell if *you specifically* peed in the pool. But you still shouldn't do it: It's bad for both you *and* your fellow swimmers. In a 2017 news release, the American Chemical Society explained: "Recent studies have shown that nitrogenous compounds (e.g., urea) in urine and sweat react with chlorine to form disinfection byproducts that can cause eye irritation and respiratory problems." You probably don't want to end a day of swimming with difficulties seeing and breathing. And perhaps more importantly, this reaction reduces the amount of chlorine in the pool, which is bad because chlorine kills off waterborne illnesses that can cause diarrhea and other maladies.

In any event, some people continue to pee between laps, regardless of the possible consequences. And scientists wanted to know just how much pee was in the average swimming pool. You can't measure the amount of urine in a pool directly, because it mixes and reacts with the rest of the water and chemicals in the pool. However, in 2017 researchers at the University of Alberta came up with an indirect way to measure, starting with something called acesulfame potassium. You may have never heard of it before, but there's a good chance you've eaten it; it's an artificial sweetener used in a lot of common products. If you want something sweet but don't want the calories from sugar, "Ace K" is an option. It delivers a sugary-sweet taste, but the human body can't process the compound, which means your body has to expunge it through your urine. And if you do your business while taking a dip in the pool, the Ace K will be left behind in the water.

Armed with this knowledge, the Canadian research team decided to test a few area pools and hot tubs for Ace K. They took samples from the pools themselves, and just to make sure the water wasn't tainted before it made its way into the basin, they also took samples from the local tap water that was typically used to fill those pools. Of the thirty-one pools surveyed, every single one showed an elevated presence of Ace K. As NPR reported, "The scientists calculated that one 220,000-gallon, commercial-size swimming pool contained almost 20 gallons of urine." To put that into context, they continued: "In a residential pool (20-by-40-foot, 5-feet deep), that would translate to about two gallons of pee."

Relatively speaking, this amount of urine is not all that much—a literal drop in the bucket. But it's still unpleasant. The typical person expels about one half of a gallon of urine each day.

Imagine collecting four days' worth of your pee, finding a pristine swimming hole, and dumping in your "collection" before going for a dip. You wouldn't do this, right? But it's basically what you're swimming in—at least in public pools.

BONUS FACT

If you do pee in the pool, you're not alone. According to a 2012 survey by the Water Quality & Health Council, 19 percent admitted to polluting a shared pool. And while he wasn't part of this survey, decorated Olympic swimmer Michael Phelps is among that 19 percent. In 2012, he told *The Wall Street Journal*, "I think everybody pees in the pool. It's kind of a normal thing to do for swimmers. When we're in the pool for two hours, we don't really get out to pee, we just go whenever we are on the wall."

FASTER THAN A SPEEDING BULLET

How Sound Affects Olympic Swimming

As of the 2016 Rio Olympic games, American swimmer Michael Phelps has twenty-eight Olympic medals to his name: twenty-three gold, three silver, and two bronze. In the 2008 Beijing Olympics alone, he set a record by winning eight gold medals, including the gold in the men's 100-meter butterfly over Milorad Cavic of Serbia. Phelps touched the wall 0.01 seconds before Cavic, and to the naked eye, discerning this difference is impossible. Even a frame-by-frame look at the finish yields little certainty. And these slight margins are not limited to swimming. For example, in the 2004 Athens Olympics, the top four finishers in the men's 100 meters finished a total of 0.04 seconds apart, with times of 9.85, 9.86, 9.87, and 9.89 seconds respectively. With margins this thin, every factor can have an impact on the outcome of an Olympic race—including the speed of sound.

At sea level, the speed of sound is about 340 meters per second. The Olympic men's 100 meters is an eight-man race, with each competitor in a roughly 1.22-meter-wide lane. The runner in Lane 1 is approximately, eight and half meters from the runner in Lane 8. If the starting pistol is fired next to Lane 1, the runner in that lane will hear it about 0.025 seconds before the runner in Lane 8. The same goes for the swimming competitions. An Olympic pool is ten lanes wide, with each lane spanning 2.5 meters. Assuming each swimmer is roughly in the middle of his or her lane, the swimmer in the first lane is about 22.5 meters away from the swimmer in the final lane. The time it takes for the sound of the starting pistol to travel from Lane 1 to Lane 10 is 0.006 seconds. And when the gap between gold and silver is less than that, it's a problem.

To solve for this issue, the Olympics (and other national competitions) wired the starting pistol to a microphone and relayed the sound to speakers situated behind each competitor in the race. The noise is relayed electronically and therefore moves much faster than the speed of sound, which should mitigate if not entirely eliminate the problem. However, going into the 2012 London Olympics, the organizers saw fit to improve this setup anyway. Why? In part, because some competitors were unwilling to trust the electronics behind them, instead "waiting" for the live sound of the pistol to reach them before starting.

As reported by *The Atlantic*, the London Olympic Games Organizing Committee decided to use the starter originally tested in the 2010 Vancouver Winter Games: an all-electronic "gun" by Omega. *Gear Patrol* explains how it works: "When the starter's finger pulls the trigger, the classic "bang" is played through speakers behind each runner's starting block [and only there], a visual flash is emitted and a pulse is sent electronically to the timing system. No smoke and the only drama is at the finish line." And as an added bonus, you don't need a permit to carry *this* gun.

BONUS FACT

Superman is said to be "faster than a speeding bullet." How fast is that? While it varies based on the specific gun, as well as the bullet, handguns generally fire between 390 and 460 meters per second. In any case, they travel—and therefore, Superman can travel—faster than the speed of sound. So, if Superman ever yells "Watch out!," he's doing the person in danger a disservice. He can reach the person faster than his voice can—assuming the sound of his voice isn't also super.

SUPERMAN TO THE RESCUE

The Comic That Saved a Family

Superman (or Clark Kent, as he preferred to be called) made his comic book debut in the first issue of *Action Comics* in June 1938. Its cover shows Superman himself, draped in his trademark red cape, lifting an exploding car, as businessmen cower and flee in terror. Despite the future popularity of the handsome superhero from planet Krypton, however, *Action Comics*, Issue 1, contains only thirteen pages of Superman comics out of a total of sixty-four pages. It also featured nine other stories, such as "The Adventures of Marco Polo," and "Scooby the Five Star Reporter" (which has nothing to do with the beloved Great Dane, Scooby-Doo).

Roughly 200,000 copies of *Action Comics*, Issue 1, were printed originally, and it retailed in the US at a cover price of 10 cents. Accounting for inflation, this would only be about $1.50 in 2019. Nowadays, a copy of *Action Comics*, Issue 1, is hard to come by, as most of the original 200,000 were discarded or lost over the succeeding decades. *Comics Buyers' Guide* notes that an estimated fifty to one hundred copies still exist, and an even smaller percentage of that amount are in decent condition. If you *can* manage to get your hands on an *Action Comics*, Issue 1, that is in top condition, however, buyers will pay handsomely. In February

2010, one such copy fetched $1 million. A month later, another copy sold for $1.5 million. And in 2011, a third copy sold for $2.16 million—easily a record in the comic book world.

Although this certainly is impressive, and fortunate for those lucky sellers, the sale of a less well-kept copy (a 5 out of 10 compared to those million-dollar copies rated 8 and up) may be more fitting of the Superman name. As reported by ABC News, a family in the American South was packing up their house for a move in the summer of 2010 when they came across a copy of *Action Comics*, Issue 1. They soon got in contact with ComicConnect.com, a marketplace and auction house that brokered the deals for the million-dollar comics. The company agreed to auction it off and noted that the comic could fetch a price as high as $250,000.

While most would be ecstatic to hear that they had found a quarter of a million dollars just sitting on a shelf and collecting dust, for this family, the discovery was more than just a windfall. The reason they were moving? Their house was in arrears and the bank was about to foreclose. Until Superman appeared, that is! ComicConnect.com contacted the bank and explained the situation. The bank agreed to hold on the foreclosure until the comic was sold. The comic ended up selling for more than $400,000, and the family was able to keep their home.

BONUS FACT

The $2.16 million paid when a copy of *Action Comics*, Issue 1, was sold did not go to a homeowner at risk of foreclosure. Most likely, it went to an insurance company. In 2000, a copy of the comic owned by actor Nicolas Cage was stolen; it turned up over a decade later, in 2011. Unfortunately Cage wasn't on the receiving end of the $2.16 million; after the theft, his insurance company paid him an estimated $1 million. It's likely that the insurance company took possession of the recovered comic and sold it to recoup the settlement cost.

KRYPTONITE AND THE KKK

When Superman Fought the Klan

In 1940, just a few years after his comic book debut, Superman took to the airwaves. For more than a decade, *The Adventures of Superman* played on radios throughout the United States, bringing the beloved Man of Steel to homes near and far. Despite being works of fiction, his story lines also mirrored things that were occurring in the real world at the time. For example, as American involvement in World War II increased, Superman regularly fought against fascism, spreading truth, justice, and the American Way from sea to shining sea.

But once the Allies had triumphed against the Nazi regime, Superman needed a new foe to battle. And one man, Stetson Kennedy, was in particular need of a hero. Kennedy was a writer who spent most of his early career documenting American folklore. In the early 1940s, Stetson, then in his twenties, had hoped to enlist in the war efforts, but back problems led the military to reject his application. Instead, he turned his efforts to fighting domestic terrorists at home—specifically, the Ku Klux Klan. Per his obituary in *The New York Times*, "Kennedy infiltrated the Klan by using the name of a deceased uncle, who had been a member, as a way to gain trust and membership." From there, he set out to expose the Klan's secrets—their tales of murder, mayhem, and other criminal activity—to the rest of the country.

Going to the authorities with his intel, though, would be a nonstarter. The Klan had become a powerful force in the American South after World War II and often, law enforcement turned a blind eye to the KKK's misdeeds (in many cases, the local authorities were Klansmen themselves). Superman, however, provided a solution to Kennedy's dilemma. Hundreds of thousands of American families were listening to each episode of his adventures, and the character was well established as a beacon of good. If Kennedy could convince Superman's radio producers to have the man from Krypton take on the Klan, perhaps the nation would turn on the KKK.

The producers were keen on the idea. Already looking for another nemesis for Superman following the end of the war, they saw the possibility to do good while also entertaining audiences. In the summer of 1946, they aired a sixteen-episode series titled "The Clan of the Fiery Cross." Referencing code words and rituals that Kennedy claimed were authentic to the Klan, Team Superman lampooned the secret society, embarrassing them to an audience of hundreds of thousands.

The Klan retaliated by calling for a boycott of the show's sponsor, Kellogg's, which used *The Adventures of Superman* to promote its bran flakes cereal, Pep. The boycott backfired. The show proved quite popular, seeing as much as a 50 percent bump in ratings in light of the controversy. As a result, the Klan suffered the opposite effect; as *Mental Floss* noted, "Within two weeks of the broadcast, KKK recruitment was down to zero." Kellogg's continued its sponsorship of the show.

BONUS FACT

Superman's weakness, kryptonite, made its public debut in *The Adventures of Superman*. Why did producers decide to give Superman an Achilles' heel? HowStuffWorks.com sums it up: "Its original purpose was to give voice actor Bud Collyer, who played the role of Superman, a vacation. With Superman incapacitated by kryptonite, another voice actor could supply moans until Collyer returned."

DOUBLE BONUS

Kellogg's is still around. They make Corn Flakes, Special K, and more than a dozen other cereals. However, Pep is long gone—and it's not hard to understand why. For years, Pep advertised itself as having "enough bran to make it mildly laxative," which didn't last as an appealing selling point.

A REVERSE APHRODISIAC

*The Curious History of Graham Crackers
and Corn Flakes*

Popular in the United States, the graham cracker is more of a cookie, typically sweetened with sugar, honey, and cinnamon. Despite their place in America's heart, however, the current recipe is a far cry from the original invention. This first recipe yielded a mild, unsweetened biscuit made of unbleached flour with bran and wheat germ added.

The creation of the original graham cracker is credited to an early 1800s Presbyterian minister by the name of Sylvester Graham, who introduced this snack item as part of a vegetarian diet that eschewed white flour and spices. Why cut out ingredients that were inherently vegetarian? Graham hoped to end what he believed to be the scourge of his time: self-pleasure. And food, he believed, was the way to do that.

Graham, one of seventeen children, believed sexual urges were something that needed to be repressed, and found "self-abuse"—a colloquialism common in the 1820s and 1830s—to be a particular ill of society. Through a combination of pseudoscience and faith, he concluded that a vegetarian diet consisting of fruits, vegetables, limited dairy, and bland starches would result in an end to lustful behavior. For the last two decades of his life, he preached that his diet, later called the Graham Diet, would help followers (called Grahamites) abstain from sexual activity—particularly from self-pleasure, which Graham argued led to insanity and blindness.

The Grahamite movement waned after its leader's death in 1851 (at the age of fifty-seven), but one man in particular stayed true to Graham's bland food (and sexual abstinence) edict. That man, Dr. John Harvey (J.H.) Kellogg, was the superintendent of the Battle Creek Sanitarium in Michigan, and he insisted that patients abide by a similar diet. He enlisted the help of Will Keith Kellogg, his brother and the sanitarium's bookkeeper, to help feed the patients, and in 1894 they invented Corn Flakes.

How this invention came about is hotly debated; per one story in the Lemelson-MIT Program's *Inventor of the Week* archive, John accidentally left out cooked wheat "for several hours." It became "softened" and "temperate," and not wanting to waste it, the Kelloggs decided to force it through the kitchen rollers to soften it for consumption. Instead, the wheat came out hard, and in a flake form. Dr. Kellogg served the flakes anyway, and they were genuinely well received by the sanitarium's patients.

The two brothers then went into business selling their new-found cereal—but their goals were very different. While Dr. Kellogg was focused on the invention's use in his practice of Graham's teachings, his brother Will had something else in mind. Will saw a mass-market opportunity for the flakes by simply adding a touch of sugar to them. This difference in ideas caused a rift between the brothers, but nevertheless, Will founded the Kellogg's corporation—now an $18 billion company. J.H. continued to focus on "rehabilitating" self-pleasurers, and without much success; by 1920, he—the very last member of the Grahamites—had all but ended his anti-sex crusade.

BONUS FACT

For a while, Oberlin College in Ohio adopted the Graham Diet, and meat, condiments, and seasonings were banned outright, even if you brought them into the dining hall yourself. One day, a professor named John P. Cowles decided to challenge the system by bringing a pepper shaker to a meal and found out that the rules were taken quite seriously: He was fired. A year or so later, student dissatisfaction with the rules culminated in a return to more typical dining hall fare.

OPERATION CORNFLAKES

How Mail Helped the Allies Win World War II

As 1945 began, war continued to rage throughout Europe. The successful D-Day landing the summer prior had given the Allies a foothold on the continent, and successful Russian campaigns in the east meant that the Nazis were fighting on both fronts. But no one was taking victory for granted; the United States and its allies continued on its campaign, hoping to force the Germans to surrender. Troops, tanks, and bombs were the thrust of these efforts—but so was propaganda. The hope was that if the Allies could convince German citizens that the war was a lost cause (or otherwise a bad idea), they would rise up against the Nazi leadership.

Delivering propaganda to an enemy's citizens is difficult, however. First, it had to actually reach its intended targets. Once there, it needed to seem credible—that is, it couldn't appear to be from an opposing nation. One easy and common method, dropping leaflets from planes, could fail both tests; dropping paper from the sky puts it at the whim of both the wind and whatever cleanup crews are waiting on the ground. Plus, who would trust a piece of paper that just dropped from the sky?

Enter US Operation Cornflakes. Part of the Allied war strategy already included attacking lines of communication, and in the 1940s, that often meant disrupting the flow of mail. Local delivery was difficult to thwart, but planes would often take aim at the railways, bombing trains which carried mail from city to city. Where possible, though, the Germans would send relief efforts to deliver whatever could be salvaged. This gave the operation's leaders an idea. In February 1945, a first wave of American planes dropped bombs on a German train, derailing it and scattering its payload. A second wave of planes followed, but they didn't drop bombs: They dropped mail. Each envelope was addressed to a real home of a real German citizen or family, and contained propaganda. The hope was that the German cleanup crew would come by, pick up all the mail—real *and* counterfeit—and deliver it.

The only question was what to put inside the envelopes. As *Mental Floss* details, "among the propaganda that arrived in German homes during the operation were *Das Neue Deutschland*, an OSS-produced newspaper that claimed to be the voice of a growing opposition party within Germany. There were also letters supposedly written by Nazi regional party leader Erich Koch discussing Hitler's poor health and generals who either wanted to surrender or take the Fuhrer out while he was weakened, creating doubt in the minds of civilians about the strength and unity of the government. Another letter, allegedly from the Verein Einsamer Kriegerfrauen (Association of Lonely War Women), was sent to German soldiers to give them the impression that it had become common for the women left at home to engage in promiscuous casual sex while they were gone, weakening their morale."

In total, Operation Cornflakes landed nearly 100,000 pieces of mail at the feet of Germans. The effectiveness of the operation is unknown—it's hard to measure, and the carnage of war meant a lot of displaced Germans weren't in their (often destroyed) homes to receive their mail anyway.

BONUS FACT

The United States military leaves no stone unturned when it comes to winning a war. A top example? The "gay bomb." In 1994, the Wright Laboratory investigated the possibility of using pheromones as a weapon against enemy troops. Specifically, the proposal requested a six-year, $7.5 million grant to see if female pheromones would cause a biological reaction among enemy troops. Ideally, the affected soldiers would find their brothers-in-arms "sexually irresistible" (per the BBC). The weapon took on the "gay bomb" moniker shortly after being discovered by a military spending watchdog group, and was never funded.

CANADA'S FRUIT MACHINE

The Pseudoscience of Discrimination

For generations, those who identified as gay or lesbian were barred from serving in the United States military. But the US was not alone in its discrimination; during the Cold War, Canada similarly purged gay men and women not only from military service but also from other civil service jobs as well. Hundreds lost their jobs, and an estimated hundreds more were demoted or otherwise adversely affected during what later became known as the "LGBT Purge." Canada's courts have since ended this practice, and in 2017 the Canadian government issued a formal apology to those affected by the Purge. This apology was also extended to those who hid their identity to avoid repercussion.

With the strides the country has taken to combat discrimination, it may be hard to believe that just fifty years earlier, the Canadian government had taken a very different approach to those who didn't attest to their sexuality: a tool called the "fruit machine." The name alone should tell you that it was up to no good. The device, developed at Carleton University by a psychologist named Frank Robert Wake, aimed to determine whether a test subject was a gay man ("fruit" being a derogatory term for such a person). The *National Post* explains: "The fruit machine consisted of a series of questions, a chair resembling one you might sit in at a dentist's office, and flashing images of mundane scenes contrasted with pornography that people in the 1950s thought gay people would like—think: half-naked carnival strongmen. Subjects (who were told the machine was measuring stress) sat in the chair and watched the images while scientists noted their pulse rate, skin reflexes, breathing rate, and pupillary response."

The science behind the machine was based on what were considered cutting-edge theories at the time. Just a few years earlier, an American researcher proposed that one could concoct a "pupillary response test" to measure involuntary reactions to visual stimuli. (That researcher, though, was focused on actual fruit: His work centered on how customers' eyes would widen slightly when something caught their attention at the grocery store.) But it was a bridge too far from science. Not only was it unlikely that images of carnival strongmen would provoke any sort of involuntary reaction, regardless of whether the subject was gay or heterosexual, but there was also no reason to presume that any such reaction would manifest in a measurable enlargement of the subject's pupils. Add in the fact that the amount of light in the room changed as different images were displayed and replaced, and the test was useless.

Canada nevertheless employed the fruit machine for more than a decade during the LGBT Purge. However, the sketchy science behind the device wasn't the reason for its ultimate retirement—the truth behind its intent was. Citizens weren't required to enter the fruit machine in order to serve in the military or in other government jobs: It was entirely optional. Regardless, many agreed to it because they thought it was merely a stress test. When the truth came out, the number of willing test subjects dropped dramatically.

BONUS FACT

Canadians are believed by many to say the word "sorry" more often than others—but don't read too much into it, especially if you're in British Columbia. In 2006, the province passed a law called the Apology Act that made it safe to say sorry without it being used legally as an admission of guilt. The main sponsor of the law, Legislative Assembly Member Lorne Mayencourt, explained to *The Globe and Mail*: "It's time for us to recognize that we've polluted the opportunity for healing by hiding behind lawyers....We need to be able to say sorry to each other for things that we've done wrong."

THE "NOT MY FAULT" BUTTON

Canada's Pin of Forgiveness

When World War II began in 1939, Canada was one of a few "autonomous Communities within the British Empire" per the 1931 Statute of Westminster, making it a mostly independent nation. While still part of the Crown, it had its own legislature and (for the most part) the right to self-rule. Canada, to reemphasize its independence, decided to wait one week before officially joining the fight; it didn't declare war on Germany until September 10. The delay didn't resonate with many of the young Canadian men and women who were eager to fight the Nazis, however. Once news hit that Britain was going to war, Canadians signed up to serve in droves, despite the fact that they were not yet under any obligation to do so.

That is, they weren't under any *legal* obligation to do so. Culturally, perhaps they were—as was true in Western Europe and would soon be true in the United States, there was an expectation at this time that if you could serve, you should. Ultimately, roughly 1.1 million Canadians served during World War II, and the vast majority did so of their own volition. Serving for Canada was a point of pride. Unless, of course, you didn't serve. In this case, the shame of cowardice could find you. In World War I, for example, a British organization "aimed to shame [British] men into enlisting in the British Army by persuading women to present them with a white feather if they were not wearing a uniform," as *The Guardian* reported; the white feather became a symbol of cowardice soon afterward. A similar specter haunted Canadian men who didn't serve in World War II, and while there wasn't a white feather, the whispers of one's neighbors served the same purpose.

But what about those citizens who were *willing* to serve but, through no fault of their own, couldn't? For example, those the military found medically unfit for service. These men and women weren't due the harassment, but were harassed nonetheless when they stayed behind while their family members, friends, and neighbors went off to war. Obviously this wasn't fair, so the Canadian government stepped in—with jewelry. Specifically, they issued a button called the "Applicant for Enlistment" pin. It came translated in both French and English, and, per Veteran Affairs Canada, was explicitly created to shield rejected applicants from the shame of not serving. The pin was made available to "[p]ersons who have voluntarily declared their unqualified willingness to serve in and beyond Canada in the Military Forces of Canada, and who are refused enlistment by reason of their not possessing, due to no faults of their own, the necessary qualifications then required for enlistment in the Naval, Army, and Air Forces of Canada."

Owning the pin meant you tried to serve but couldn't, and were in no way a coward (at least not when it came to the war). And if you didn't earn it and were caught with it? It came with a $500 fine (in Canadian dollars), which is close to $8,000 Canadian dollars as of 2019. Whether the button successfully delivered on its mission, though, is mostly unknown; Canada didn't start issuing it until the fall of 1941, and some undeserving citizens were surely harangued during that two-year period.

> ## BONUS FACT
>
> During the course of World War II, Canada declared war on Germany, Italy, Finland, Hungary, Romania, and Japan. These were the first times Canada had ever made a formal declaration of war—and, as of 2019, the last times as well, as Canada has not declared war since.

WHO'S SORRY NOW?

A Professional Apology

At the end of 2013, the United States Department of Transportation released its monthly ranking of airlines based on on-time performance. It was bad news for Southwest Airlines, which had now come in last on the list for two straight months. The methodology used to make this determination was somewhat controversial—the inspector general of the agency has stated as much—but if you're an air traveler whose flight was delayed significantly, that's hardly any solace. But that's okay. When it comes to apologies and explanations, Southwest had a guy for that. His name was Fred Taylor, and it was his job to be sorry that your flight didn't work out as planned.

From May 1997 until the summer of 2001, Taylor was working as an assistant customer service manager out of one of Southwest's smaller offices in Baltimore, Maryland. The president of the corporation at the time, Colleen Barrett, took notice of him and handpicked him for a new role leading up what the company called "proactive customer service." This is not a typical title, and therefore requires a bit of additional explaining. Fortunately, a

2007 profile in *The New York Times* summed up Taylor's unique job duties nicely, reporting that he "spends his 12-hour work days finding out how Southwest disappointed its customers and then firing off homespun letters of apology." The *Times* half-jokingly called Taylor the airline's "chief apology officer."

The apology letters he wrote weren't form letters. They all followed a similar format, sure, but they responded to the customer's specific issues. As *The Dallas Morning News* reported, each letter contained a sincere apology, an explanation as to what went wrong and why, and a voucher to defray some of the cost of a future flight with Southwest. In the letter, Taylor's team investigated what occurred on the flight in question and detailed the reasons behind it. In one example, *The Dallas Morning News* cited a flight where a female passenger inexplicably "kneeled in front of her middle seat and chewed on the seat cushion, then stripped off her top and ran down the aisle." Taylor sent an apology to the other travelers on board (not that the woman's bizarre behavior was at all the airline's fault) within twenty-four hours.

This may sound commonplace in the customer service world, but what made Taylor and his team unique is that they didn't wait for customers to complain. Instead, once Taylor found out about a problem—typically early on in the process, and often from the flight crew itself—he issued the apology letter and voucher to all passengers involved. This was true whether the problems were caused by another customer, the weather, or an error on Southwest's own part.

Some watchdogs took notice of Taylor's work too. *Consumerist*—typically a consumer advocate that focuses on the negatives within different corporations—cited one of Taylor's team's letters with approval, calling it "refreshingly honest and informative." Whether his proactive approach was ultimately successful is hard to say, but there is one sign that heavily suggests that it is: At least four other airlines—American, JetBlue, Continental (pre-United merger), and US Airways—have experimented with similar approaches. As of 2015, Taylor is no longer Southwest's apologizer in chief; he transitioned to a new role with the company at that time.

BONUS FACT

Those fluent in stock market matters may believe that Southwest's customer-first approach is in its DNA—or, more accurately, its ticker symbol. Southwest trades on the New York Stock Exchange under the symbol LUV, an obvious reference to love. In this case, however, love is not in the air: It's on the ground. LUV is a reference to Dallas's Love Field Airport, which was the main airport in the area until Dallas/Fort Worth International opened in 1974, and was Southwest's first hub.

HAM TAKES TO THE SKIES

How Pigs Stopped Birds from Damaging Airplanes

On January 15, 2009, US Airways Flight 1549 took off from LaGuardia Airport in New York on its way to Seattle. It didn't get very far. As the plane made its ascent, a flock of Canada geese struck the plane, taking out its engines. Fortunately, the pilots—Chesley Sullenberger and Jeffrey Skiles—were somehow able to glide the plane safely into the Hudson River. While one hundred of the one hundred and fifty-five passengers and crew on board suffered injuries, there were no fatalities. The accident was dubbed the "Miracle on the Hudson," a testament to the crew's quick thinking under pressure.

While the events of that day are an extreme example of what can go wrong, bird-related aircraft accidents are hardly rare. According to a Federal Aviation Administration (FAA) report from 2016, there are approximately 13,000 such incidents in the US annually. The vast majority of these bird strikes are harmless (if a seagull goes up against a plane hull, the bird is going to lose) but the exceptions require countermeasures. Even if no one is hurt, if a bird hits a plane just right, it can cause hundreds of thousands of dollars of damage and require that the plane make an emergency landing. Airports typically employ loudspeakers and pyrotechnics to disrupt bird colonies that may affect a plane, but there's no substitute for keeping the populations under control in the first place. Sometimes that's simply impossible: In the case of Flight 1549, one can't just prevent Canada geese from migrating up the Atlantic coast. In some cases however, airports can take action to relocate a flock.

One great example involved a hunting club in Salt Lake City. In 1999, the club established a colony of about 10,000 gulls on an island north of Salt Lake City's airport. At the time, no one realized how bad this was. According to the airport's "wildlife hazard management plan," the birds' daily flight pattern became a path "directly over the airport's center and east runways." This required a creative intervention. Step one was straightforward: Remove the nests. However, this proved to be a temporary solution, as the gulls returned to the island to lay more eggs. They then tried something called "egg addling." The mother gulls were scared off the island and, while they were away, wildlife management covered the temporarily abandoned eggs in vegetable oil. Per the *Deseret News*, this "blocks oxygen and prevents the eggs from hatching." Some gulls learned that their eggs wouldn't hatch on the island, so they moved on to other habitats—but there were holdouts. So Salt Lake City brought in the pigs.

Pigs are voracious and indiscriminate eaters; in other words, they'll eat just about anything—and eggs are most certainly on that list. So, airport officials brought some in to finish off the job. Per the BBC, the animals "trampled and ate the gulls' eggs." And this solution has staying power. The BBC continued: "[Pigs] are now used for a few weeks every spring as a deterrent. The migrating gulls arrive, see the pigs waiting to eat their eggs, and then go to another location." As it turns out, while pigs don't fly, they *can* help people take to the skies more safely.

BONUS FACT

Pigs aren't the only creative anti-bird tool used by aviation officials. In 2004, Chicago's O'Hare International Airport sprayed the chemical used in artificial grape flavoring—the stuff you'd find in bubble gum, cough medicine, and grape Kool-Aid—around the premises. Why? Birds really hate it. Richard Dolbeer, then the national coordinator of airport wildlife services at the US Department of Agriculture, explained the theory to the *Chicago Tribune*: "The grape flavoring acts as a repellent, like a bird tear gas."

THE GIMLI GLIDER

How a Unit Conversion Error Made the Skies a Little Less Friendly

A flight from Montreal to Edmonton is about 1,800 miles or 2,900 kilometers long. As you probably already knew, these distances are the same, just with a different unit of measure. But getting the units of measure wrong can cause problems—as Air Canada Flight 143 discovered firsthand.

Most of the world uses the metric system (meters, liters, and grams), while a few countries (the US, Liberia, and Myanmar) use the "customary" or "imperial" system: feet, gallons, and pounds. Canada was one of the latter countries until 1970, when the nation began to change to the metric system. The full process of changing over took about fifteen years, with one of the last industries to change over being airlines (which, given the expense and longevity of the equipment makes sense).

On July 23, 1983, Air Canada Flight 143 was one of the earliest flights to use the new metric units. Unfortunately, Air Canada was also undergoing a second change at the same time: smaller flight crews. Typically, there were three core members of the crew: the pilot, copilot, and flight engineer. Flight 143, though, didn't have a flight engineer, so the preflight fueling protocol fell to the pilot and copilot. This protocol required them to convert volume (liters) into mass (kilograms) in order to figure out how much additional fuel was needed for the flight. They did exactly that—except they got the labels wrong. Instead of figuring out how many liters of fuel the plane needed to hit the required amount of 22,300 *kilograms*, the crew calculated how many liters were needed to hit 22,300 *pounds*. Because of this error, they ended up with 10,100 kilograms of fuel—about half the amount required to reach their destination.

Having half the fuel needed, of course, means you're only getting halfway to your destination, which—when the vehicle in question is an airplane cruising 12,500 meters (41,000 feet) above the ground—is a problem. The onboard computer (which was fed the wrong data) didn't give them warning until it was too late. The left-side engine died, then the right, and because most of the plane's flight instruments were powered by a fuel-driven electrical system, those soon went dark too. The plane was going down.

Luckily, the pilot and copilot were better at flying than math. As *The New York Times* reported after the incident, the pilot had ten years of glider training under his belt, and his copilot had trained at RCAF Station Gimli during his days with the Canadian Air Force, so he knew the surroundings quite well. Together, they were able to land the plane—gliding the last 100 km (60 miles)—touching down just an hour or so before nightfall. The plane (the Gimli Glider, as it would henceforth be known) suffered some damage to its nose, and a few tires were blown out, but the passengers were safe. Ten people suffered minor injuries, but there were no fatalities.

BONUS FACT

If you wanted to own the Gimli Glider, you could have—if you were willing to fork over about $2.75 million (in Canadian dollars). The plane was decommissioned in 2008 and put up for auction in February 2013, expecting to land a price near (or in excess of) that amount. Surprisingly, the top bid came to only $425,000 (in Canadian dollars), which wasn't enough to meet the plane's reserve price. Unsold, the plane was dismantled in 2014.

PIRATING MEASUREMENTS

How the Jolly Roger Hijacked
the Metric System

Throughout most of the world, people use the metric system (meters, liters, grams) as their units of measure. However, a few nations, most notably the United States, don't use the metric system in everyday life. Instead, they employ what is known as the "imperial system," which uses units such as miles, pounds, and gallons. When it comes to cars, for example, the speedometer shows American drivers how fast they are going in "miles per hour," and the road signs use the same units to tell them if that's too fast. Scales use "pounds," gasoline is sold by the "gallon," and so on.

So why exactly does the US use a different system? Blame pirates. In the country's early days (the late 1700s), it was a hodgepodge of different states and cultures all under one federal government. And when it came to interstate commerce, these regional peculiarities made things difficult—specifically, the differences in weights and measures. The official "pound" used in New York, for example, may have weighed a different amount than the one used in, say, Virginia, and neither was in a position to force the other to adjust its standards. In January 1790, in his first-ever

State of the Union address, President George Washington made specific note of this problem, stating that "uniformity in the currency, weights, and measures of the United States is an object of great importance, and will, I am persuaded, be duly attended to." That wasn't an idle wish, either; his secretary of state, Thomas Jefferson, got to work on a solution.

Among the various options that Jefferson proposed was a base-ten system, which would break everything down into divisions and multiples of ten. For example, an inch would be one tenth of one foot and one mile would be 10,000 feet. This idea had the support of George Washington, James Madison, and Alexander Hamilton, but Congress was slow to act, failing to adopt it by the time 1790 had ended. Jefferson, however, did not give up.

France was also working on a decimal system of its own at this time—the one now known as the metric system. Jefferson wrote to his French contacts to inquire about this new "metric" system, hoping that unified weights and measures could not only benefit interstate trade but also international trade. To move this process along, France dispatched a scientist named Joseph Dombey to the United States in 1793. With him was a small metallic cylinder with what looked like a handle on top. This cylinder was the official "kilogram," and weighed one kilogram. This was the weight by which other weights were measured: The basis for measuring mass using the metric system.

It should have been simple: Dombey would give the kilogram to Jefferson; Jefferson would propose the metric system to Congress; Congress would most likely endorse the system; and the US would still use this system today. But that didn't happen—because the kilogram never got to Jefferson. Ocean winds blew Dombey's ship off course; instead of landing safely near Washington, DC, it sailed into the Caribbean Sea. There, British privateers—basically pirates, but with permission of the

Crown to raid non-British ships with impunity—boarded and looted Dombey's vessel. They imprisoned Dombey, who (per *The Washington Post*) lived out the rest of his life under lock and key, and they auctioned off whatever seemed valuable from his ship. This included the official kilogram, which ultimately ended up in what is now the National Institute of Standards and Technology. France did dispatch another scientist with another official kilogram that arrived safely, but by then Jefferson was no longer secretary of state and his successor showed little interest in systems of weight and measures.

BONUS FACT

Want to be a pirate? This is generally a bad idea, as they're considered criminals, but there's one exception should you get into the Massachusetts Institute of Technology. If you pass classes in archery, fencing, pistol or rifle, and sailing at MIT, the Physical Education & Wellness Office will also grant you a "Pirate Certificate." The office's website does warn, however, that "the MIT Pirate certificate is for entertainment purposes only and does not give the recipient license to engage in piracy or any pirate activities."

THE BILLS GO MARCHING, TWO BY TWO

Thomas Jefferson's Silent Armies

Thomas Jefferson was the primary author of the Declaration of Independence, the first secretary of state of the United States, and its third president. He's depicted on Mount Rushmore along with George Washington, Abraham Lincoln, and Theodore Roosevelt. If you live in the United States, you probably have a few images of him lying around as well; just check your pockets: He's on the nickel. He's also on the two-dollar bill, but it's unlikely you have one of those at the ready, because they're not so common. While two-dollar bills are still in circulation, they make up less than 1 percent of the bills produced each year. Retail cash registers also don't typically have slots for them, and if you get one as change, it'd be surprising to say the least. In many cases, banks do not even carry them. In short, two-dollar bills certainly exist, but you'd hardly know it—which makes them an effective protest tool.

Throughout history, there are many examples of groups of people feeling neglected or taken for granted. In many cases, the impact of that group on the local economy is significant, but hard to quantify, and even harder to see. To fix this, consider grabbing a large pile of Jeffersons. The idea is simple: First, gather a group of people who support a common cause. Next, have them patronize local businesses, paying only in cash, and with two-dollar bills wherever possible. Eventually, stores will have to give the two-dollar bills to other customers as change, and as the bills spread, so will the bemused puzzlement of the townsfolk: Where did all these two-dollar bills come from? Finally, you will take to the area's newspaper to explain, demonstrating your group's impact on the local economy.

This is by no means an original idea, though. This tactic has been used for decades, and by many different groups. One of the earliest examples was cited by syndicated financial columnist Sylvia Porter in 1964 (notable because the two-dollar bill would be discontinued just two years later, until being reintroduced in 1976 for the US bicentennial). In this example, military bases threatened with closure advised soldiers stationed there to use two-dollar bills at businesses in the area. Unfortunately, the scheme failed at this time because bills of that denomination were often considered a bad omen, and downstream recipients would either refuse them or otherwise make them disappear.

In 1977—just a year after the currency's reintroduction—the two-dollar bill tactic was also used by football enthusiasts. Georgia Tech in Atlanta and Clemson University in South Carolina were football rivals, playing at each other's stadiums in alternating years. For some reason, Georgia Tech suddenly refused to travel north, and in response, Clemson announced that the 1977 game in Atlanta would be the final one between the schools. A Clemson booster encouraged fans traveling to the game to spend two-dollar bills to show the revenue that the area would lose out on in the future. While the story made the press, it's hard to say if it worked, as the rivalry between the teams resumed in 1983.

Nevertheless, many others have tried the same type of economic-signaling marketing campaign. Examples range from the strange (e.g., participants at a barbershop quartet convention, skydivers, and nudists have all employed the tactic) to the more serious and politically charged. In any event, the next time someone hands you back your change with a two-dollar bill in it, there may be an interesting reason why.

BONUS FACT

If you get a lot of two-dollar bills, don't spend them all at once. In 2005, a Maryland-area man named Mike Bolesta ordered a new car stereo for his son from Best Buy. Due to a mix-up, the store initially waived the installation charges but later demanded the $114 fee. Bolesta, who gave away two-dollar bills as part of his tour guide business, attempted to pay with fifty-seven two-dollar bills. They assumed the bills were fake and called the police. Bolesta was arrested, and the Secret Service was called in before he was released.

SPRINTING FOR OFFICE

The Political Race That Was Literally a Race

When John Adams, the second President of the United States, died on July 4, 1826, his last words were "Thomas Jefferson still survives." This wasn't quite right, as Jefferson had died earlier that day. But he wasn't making a joke: He was making peace with Jefferson, who had been a bitter political rival. With that, tension was laid to rest in Washington. Unfortunately that wouldn't be the case more than a century later.

In 1932, a Democrat named Clarence D. Martin handily won Washington's gubernatorial election; he and his running mate, fellow Democrat Vic Meyers, took office the following January. Almost immediately, Martin made enemies within his own party, as he appointed Republicans to cabinet posts in an effort to use bipartisanship to combat the Great Depression. He adopted more moderate policies than many Democrats hoped and earned a reputation for being one of the more conservative members of his party (he was popular with the voters, however, earning re-election four years later).

But those on the more liberal side of the party did find themselves an ally—in Lieutenant Governor Meyers. In general, lieutenant governors are about as powerful as vice presidents (which is to say, hardly at all). As long as the governor was around, Lieutenant Governor Meyers could speak his mind, but he couldn't enact policy changes. Washington took "being around" pretty seriously, however; when Governor Martin was out of state, Meyers had actual power. He could call the legislature back into session and sign into law anything that they passed that he liked.

In 1938, this is exactly what those more progressive politicians tried to get him to do. In April of that year, Martin went on a cross-country trip to Washington, DC, on state business. This wasn't a vacation, but it was good enough for those who wanted to push a different agenda. They asked Meyers to call the legislature back into session, which he was willing to do. There was a problem, however: He, too, was out of state. In fact, he had just left for vacation in California. *HistoryLink* describes what happened next: "[Meyers] caught a train as far as Portland; got a ride from the Portland police to Vancouver; commandeered a state patrol car to Seattle. He needed to be in [the state capital,] Olympia, so the secretary of state could attest his proclamation, so he chartered a plane but arrived after the office had closed for the day. He went back to Seattle and announced over [Seattle radio station] KOL that he intended to call a special session."

The people in his own state weren't the only ones to hear this radio announcement: so did Governor Martin. In response, Martin chartered a private plane at his own expense (there were no commercial flights available that late at night), hoping to arrive back home before his second-in-command could usurp his power. But, by the time Martin landed, Meyers had already submitted a proclamation calling for a special session, and it looked like the ruse had worked. The state supreme court thought otherwise.

Per *The New York Times*, the court noted that "Governor Martin's plane flew across the boundary between Idaho and Washington only thirteen minutes before" Meyers issued his proclamation. As a result, the court ruled, the proclamation was a nullity. Martin also asked the state legislature to change the rules going forward, which they ultimately did.

BONUS FACT

One of the names originally proposed for the state of Washington was "Columbia," after the Columbia River, the major internal waterway of the area. Leaders, however, thought better of the name; the capital of the nation was already named the "District of Columbia," and that could lead to confusion. They aimed to alleviate confusion by naming the state "Washington" instead. Of course, that hasn't worked either.

THE SENATOR RESTS

A State Senate Showdown with
a Surprise Ending

For most of 2000, the United States was focused on the presidential election, which was headlined by Vice President Al Gore and Texas Governor George W. Bush. But this wasn't the only political race that year—and it almost certainly wasn't the nastiest.

In Missouri, voters were tasked with electing a senator that year to represent them in Washington. The incumbent, Republican John Ashcroft, was likely the favorite going into the election. He had won the election six years prior in a landslide, taking 59.7 percent of the votes to his Democratic opponent's 35.7 percent. Further, Ashcroft had a sizeable war chest to fund his campaign and could ride the coattails of Bush, who appeared primed to win the state. But Ashcroft's opponent that year was a popular politician in his own right: incumbent Governor Mel Carnahan. Like Ashcroft, Carnahan won the office he then held with relative ease; he was originally elected in 1992 by seventeen points, and won re-election four years later by roughly the same margin.

Most experts believed Ashcroft would prevail, and, like in any tight race, they expected this one to be particularly nasty, as both major party candidates would try to cut out the other's support. This prediction came true. Though what the experts didn't account for was what happened on the evening of October 16, 2000—the night before one of the senate debates. That night, Carnahan and his campaign manager were aboard a small plane piloted by Carnahan's son. It crashed, killing all three men aboard. When reporting the crash, *The Washington Post* also pointed out what appeared obvious: "The tragedy greatly reduces Democratic hopes to take control of the Senate."

Ashcroft immediately paused his campaign. Not only would it be unseemly to ask for votes right after such a tragedy, he also didn't have an opponent anymore—or so it seemed. Because the election was only three weeks away, Missouri law prevented new candidates from joining the race; Mel Carnahan, despite being deceased, would remain on the ballot. Missouri voters were left with a choice between Ashcroft, the deceased Carnahan, and a third-party candidate.

The late Democratic nominee also posed an odd problem. A deceased person can't take the oath of office and clearly can't be a senator—but what if he or she were to win anyway? If you treat the situation like any other senate vacancy, it falls to the state governor to appoint a new senator until a special election can be held. In that case, if Carnahan were to win, the seat would be vacant as of January 3, 2001. Missouri was about to elect a new governor, who would take office January 8, 2001, meaning the current governor would have an opportunity to appoint a senator. Upon Carnahan's death, his lieutenant governor, Democrat Roger B. Wilson, became that person—and he had an idea.

A few days after Carnahan's death, Wilson announced that he would nominate Carnahan's widow, Jean Carnahan, if the late governor were to win. The election quickly approaching, Ashcroft resumed his campaign but was hamstrung by the events of the days prior. While Ashcroft's attack ads may have been effective when Carnahan was alive, they'd almost certainly backfire now. Not only had the late Mel Carnahan's reputation been rehabilitated by his death, but sullying his name to prevent his grieving widow from taking office would have been a bad political move. The final days of campaigning were tepid and uncharacteristically polite. Ultimately, Mel Carnahan won, taking 50.5 percent of the votes to Ashcroft's 48.4 percent.

BONUS FACT

If you had to make a list of the most famous people from Missouri, neither Ashcroft nor Carnahan would likely make the list—but a guy named Samuel Clemens would. In his early twenties, Clemens found work as an apprentice steamboat pilot on the Mississippi River. This experience left a lasting impression on him: his nom de plume, Mark Twain. "Mark twain" is riverboat lingo used to announce that a ship has reached the necessary depth of twelve feet in order to operate. "Twain" is Old English for "two"; "mark" referred to the fact that the measuring tool had hit the second mark, with each mark measuring six feet.

A BESTSELLING GHOST WRITER

The Mark Twain Novel You Hopefully Skipped

When Mark Twain died on April 21, 1910, the world lost a prolific author. Over the course of his seventy-five years, he wrote more than two dozen short stories and almost as many books (a number of them being left unfinished); as MarkTwainMuseum.org explains, "the number depends on one's distinction between what is a short book or a long short story." While the total count is ambiguous, one thing is almost certainly true: He didn't write anything after he died. Again, that's *almost* certainly.

To be clear, books and stories written by Twain *were* published posthumously. In fact, the first comprehensive publishing of his autobiography wasn't until 2010, an entire century after his death, as per Twain's own instructions. What is an issue, however, is whether he wrote anything new after he passed away. In 1917, if you were to ask a woman named Emily Grant Hutchings for her opinion on the matter, she would have unequivocally stated that Twain kept writing even after his death. She knew this because he dictated a book to her via a Ouija board—at least, that is what she claimed.

The book Twain allegedly dictated to her is titled *Jap Herron*. It is the story of a boy born into poverty in Missouri who overcomes his lot in life to become an upstanding member of society, bringing his town to better footing in the process. Critics agreed that regardless of who wrote it, it wasn't very good. *The New York Times* reviewed the book in September of that year, concluding that "if this is the best that 'Mark Twain' can do by reaching across the barrier, the army of admirers that his works have won for him will all hope that he will hereafter respect that boundary." Regardless of the writing quality, however, Ouija boards were popular at the time and Hutchings's publisher, Mitchell Kennerley, wasn't about to pass up the chance to get a final story from the famed author on shelves.

Twain's estate felt otherwise. His daughter Clara Clemens and his former publisher sued. The claim: copyright and trademark infringement. According to them, if the ghost of Mark Twain really did dictate the story to Hutchings, she was a mere stenographer; Twain's estate would own the copyright to the story. Additionally, Twain's publisher had trademarked the "Mark Twain" nom de plume, so using it without the publisher's permission was a violation of their trademark.

Hutchings was stuck. If she continued to claim that the disembodied Twain wrote the book, she'd likely lose this lawsuit; if she said the initial claim was untrue, however...well, who wants to buy a bad book not written by Mark Twain? The two parties ended up settling. Mitchell Kennerley and Hutchings agreed to stop publishing the book and destroyed the existing copies as best they could. The ghost of Mark Twain, as far as anyone knows, has yet to be heard from again.

BONUS FACT

As mentioned previously, the first volume of Mark Twain's autobiography wasn't published until 2010. Despite the delay and the fact that it was a hefty read (totaling well over seven hundred pages), it was a bestseller. As a result, Twain had bestselling books debut in the nineteenth, twentieth, and twenty-first centuries.

A GHASTLY WITNESS

*How a Ouija Board Can Protect
You from a Lawsuit*

Looking to solve the mystery of the posthumous Twain novel for yourself? You could try a consumer favorite: the Ouija board. This mass-produced "game" is basically a wooden plank with the letters of the alphabet, numbers zero to nine, and words "yes," "no," and "goodbye" printed on it. It comes with a little heart-shaped piece of plastic or wood called a "planchette," which purportedly focuses the energy of those who touch it. When the users place their hands on the planchette, it moves, powered by the spirit of a deceased person (so they say), to answer questions users ask that spirit. The power of these devices is primarily up to consumer discretion, but in 1921, Chicago had to make sure that twelve specific men were willing to swear, under penalty of perjury, that they didn't believe in Ouija-powering ghosts.

Before late 1919, two couples—the Yosts and the Walters— were friends who spent time together fairly regularly. However, as the *Chicago Tribune* noted, that relationship went south when Mrs. Walter ran for a leadership role in their local community group. She expected Mrs. Yost to support her efforts but found the opposite was true; Mrs. Yost ran against her—and won. An upset Mrs. Walter decided to investigate. It turned out that the Yosts' home had been burgled on the night of November 10, 1919. The thief, per the *Tribune*, "looted of a small sum of money, a bunch of groceries, and 25 pounds of raisins" and became the buzz of the town. Unfortunately the identity of the culprit remained unknown—until Thanksgiving. That night, the Yosts broke out a Ouija board while hosting other friends. One of the guests asked the Ouija board who robbed the Yost home, and the planchette apparently spelled out "the Walter family." News of the paranormal confession spread, and her now-besmirched reputation likely caused Mrs. Walter to lose the election.

So, the Walters sued. In general, you can't accuse people of crimes without running the risk of liability, and the Walters demanded compensation for their sullied names. The lawsuit demanded a hefty $10,000 in damages—the equivalent of more than $125,000 dollars in 2018. Needless to say, the Yosts weren't keen on paying this. They came up with a creative defense, arguing that Mrs. Yost didn't make any defamatory statements against the Walters: It was the Ouija board.

To determine whether the Yosts were liable for damages, the court needed to account for the possibility that jurors would attribute the statement to the unexplained. As the *New York Tribune* explained, at least six prospective jurors were dismissed because they were too willing to believe that ghosts were real. The case eventually proceeded, as the *Tribune* described, with a jury of "twelve good men and true who are sure that no such thing as a spirit world exists and that Ouija boards are merely something with which to while away time."

But the Ouija board wasn't out of the picture yet. According to the *Independence Daily Reporter*, the judge "instructed the jury that if Mrs. Yost said the Ouija board had revealed Mrs. Walter as the alleged robber, Mrs. Yost was not guilty" but "if Mrs. Yost made the remarks herself, however, and neglected to quote Ouija," the Walters could collect. The jury found that Mrs. Yost cited the Ouija board every time she mentioned Mrs. Walter's role in the theft, and the Walters lost to what was perhaps the world's first-ever successful "defense by Ouija board."

BONUS FACT

Why steal 25 pounds of raisins? And, in the case of the Yosts, why have 25 pounds of raisins in the first place? Today, you probably wouldn't, but as 1920 approached, so did Prohibition. And if you have enough raisins, you're on your way to making a type of moonshine called "raisin jack." While the newspapers didn't spell it out, chances are the Yosts (and the real thieves) were planning to make some illicit spirits in their spare time.

JUDGING A JUDGE
BY HIS COVER

A Creative Way to Claim the Luck of the Irish

In 2010, a criminal defense and bankruptcy attorney named Phillip Spiwak ran in a Republican primary for an open judicial seat in Will County, Illinois. The winner would almost certainly become the next judge in the area; the Democrats didn't even bother fielding a candidate. However, Spiwak ended up coming in third, taking only 11 percent of the vote. Eight years later, a criminal defense and bankruptcy attorney named Shannon O'Malley ran, as a Democrat, for a judicial seat in nearby Cook County, Illinois.

These elections seem unrelated at first glance. Sure, the highlighted candidates had similar legal practices, but that's where the similarities ended. One was a Republican from Will County with a Polish-sounding name; the other, a Democrat from Cook County with an Irish-sounding name. However, if you looked at a picture of Phillip Spiwak next to one of Shannon O'Malley, you'd think they were twins. They're not: They're the same person.

People change their names all the time, so on the surface this may not be so unusual. And Spiwak had a seemingly plausible explanation for his new identity; he told NBC News that he "changed [his] name out of respect for [his] mentor and surrogate father, who passed away due to cancer." Perhaps this was the truth—but cynics had another theory. They believed that O'Malley (nee Spiwak) changed his name to earn himself extra votes.

Cook County has a longstanding history of preferring candidates with Irish-sounding names. In October 1990, long before Mr. O'Malley won himself a judgeship, *The New York Times* noted this phenomenon. In an article titled, "Where an Irish Name Wins Everyone's Vote," the newspaper opened with a joke: "This is the County of Cook, not Cork. And contrary to rumor, the election ballots in Illinois next month will not be printed in Gaelic." Candidates with traditionally Irish names, the *Times* went on to explain, tended to fare better than those with non-Irish names. So, "over the years, more than one candidate for judge here has legally changed names to sound Irish." Similarly, as reported the *Chicago Tribune*, "a 2011 DePaul University study found that having the only Irish woman's name in a [Cook County] judicial race is worth more than a party slating."

This voter bias was so common that in 2007, the state legislature passed a law in response. Under the new law, if you changed your name within three years before the deadline to get onto a ballot, your old name would appear on the ballot alongside your new one, with the words "formerly known as" attached. This didn't stop the former Mr. Spiwak: He changed his name in September 2010, well before the 2018 election.

The *Tribune*, though, didn't think much of the maneuver. The newspaper summed up their pre-election coverage by concluding that "alas, for O'Malley, the seat is routinely won by Republicans. In a down-ballot race in which voters typically vote strictly on party lines, his name change in [*sic*] unlikely to be enough. 'Tis a shame!" They were wrong, however: It was a close election, but O'Malley triumphed, earning 57,778 votes to Republican Daniel Patrick Fitzgerald's 55,500.

BONUS FACT

Every year on the Saturday before Saint Patrick's Day (or on Saint Patrick's Day itself whenever it falls on a Saturday), the city of Chicago famously turns its river green. The tradition wasn't originally in honor of the city's Irish population, though. According to a 2003 *UWire* report, "the idea of dyeing the Chicago River green originally came about by accident when a group of plumbers were using green dye to trace illegal substances that were polluting the river." Today, the dyeing of the river is sponsored by the local plumbers union.

THE BIGGEST NAMES IN SHOWBIZ

How to Guarantee Your Show Gets Great Reviews

When Broadway producer David Merrick died in April 2000, the obituaries sang his praises. Merrick was one of his industry's most decorated; over his thirty-plus-year career, he won eleven Tony Awards, including ones for *Hello, Dolly!* and *42nd Street.* But most obituaries also spent a lot of ink on one of his failures: a 1961 musical comedy called *Subways Are for Sleeping.* If you're not familiar with the play, don't worry: It's hardly well known, mostly because it stumbled out of the gate. The advertising campaign was a dud; at the time, bus and subway advertising was a key to any media buy, and New York's transit authority rejected ads for the play because it was about vagrants using the subway system as a motel. Unfortunately, the reviews of the show were also mixed to mostly negative, making it even harder for Merrick to drum up interest. So, Merrick faked it—kind of.

On January 4, 1962, the now-defunct *New York Herald Tribune* ran a full-page ad promoting the musical. The headline declared that "7 Out of 7 Are Ecstatically Unanimous About *Subways Are for Sleeping.*" The ad featured the names of seven well-known theater critics at the time, and next to each of their names was a line of unmitigated praise. For example, per the ad, Howard

Taubman called *Subways* "one of the few great musical comedies of the last 30 years" and "one of the best of our time." If you were in the theater industry at the time, you immediately recognized Taubman's name: He was the critic for *The New York Times*.

However, if you knew the *Times* critic personally, you would have also noticed that something was off: The picture of Taubman in the ad wasn't actually a picture of him. Friends of the other critics featured in the ad would have noticed the same thing. For example, according to *The Museum of Hoaxes*, one newspaper editor noticed that "the picture of Richard Watts showed a black man," which couldn't be right, as "the editor knew that Richard Watts, the theater critic, was white." The ad appeared to be a total lie, and other newspapers throughout the area rejected it. The *Herald Tribune* was the lone exception and solely because it went to print before anyone noticed. It seemed as though Merrick's lie had failed.

It wasn't a lie, though: It was a PR stunt. And the stunt wasn't a failure. According to *The New York Times*, Merrick didn't ask the critics for reviews; instead, he consulted the phone book. He found seven men with the same names as the critics—"among them a mailman and a shoe salesman," per the *Times*—and treated them to a preview of the show, along with a free dinner. These seven "winners" returned the favor by giving Merrick the glowing reviews he was after. It didn't matter that most of the newspapers rejected the ad: The details of the scheme became international news. Per the *Times*, the buzz around Merrick's stunt "was enough to garner international headlines and keep *Subways* on the boards for a nearly profitable season."

Ultimately, *Subways Are for Sleeping* wasn't strong enough to make it any further on its own. It ran for just six months, totaling 205 performances. As meager as that sounds, however, it would have been far fewer had it not been for the publicity derived from Merrick's stunt.

BONUS FACT

If you saw *The Real Thing* on Broadway in 1984, you likely noticed the name Cynthia Nixon in your *Playbill*. And if you saw the show *Hurlyburly* the next night, you'd have seen the same name listed. This wasn't a scam like Merrick's, however: It was an incredible acting feat. Nixon, a college freshman at the time (now best known for playing Miranda in *Sex and the City*), had a small part in both shows—even though they were on Broadway simultaneously. The theaters were close enough to one another that she could run back and forth as needed.

A WARRANTED MISTAKE

If the Description Fits, You Must...Acquit?

On February 2, 1958, a man named Roberto Hernandez was born in Tijuana, Mexico. He later moved to the Los Angeles area and, just weeks after his twenty-eighth birthday, had a run-in with the law. On February 26, 1986, Hernandez—about 5'8" tall and weighing roughly 160 pounds, with brown hair and a tattoo on his left harm—landed a job and celebrated an end to a long spell of unemployment by downing a few beers. As he was heading home, Inglewood, California, police pulled him over for driving drunk. He failed a field sobriety test and was arrested, spending the night in jail.

The next morning, Hernandez expected to be released. He wasn't. Instead, the police told him that there was an outstanding warrant for his arrest. As they informed the judge, Roberto Hernandez was arrested on September 25, 1985, in Chicago as he was about to break into someone else's house. Hernandez was never brought to trial, though: He jumped bail instead. From that point on, there was a warrant out for his arrest listed in the national crime database. And while there are a lot of Roberto Hernandezes in the United States, the rest of the description for this wanted man was 5'8" tall, brown hair, tattoo on left arm, 160 pounds." Additionally, his birth date was February 2, 1958.

Suffice it to say that on February 26, 1986, Roberto Hernandez found himself in a lot of trouble. His excuse, as he recounted to *People* magazine: "I've never been to Chicago. I've never been east of Las Vegas." No one was buying it. Not only did the names, birthdates, and descriptions match, but eight of the nine digits in Hernandez's Social Security number were the same as that of the man the Chicago authorities were after. The Inglewood police didn't believe him when he claimed that it was a case of mistaken identity. As a result, Hernandez spent the next eleven days in jail as California and Illinois worked out his extradition—and he was fired from the job he had just landed.

Despite this, he wasn't brought to Chicago to answer for his crimes. Instead, he was released without an explanation. He didn't need one, however, because he knew the truth: There really were two Roberto Hernandezes born on February 2, 1958, matching the same description, and with very similar Social Security numbers. And the one in custody outside Los Angeles wasn't the burglar that Chicago was looking for.

The *mostly* innocent Hernandez (he was, after all, guilty of drunk driving) sued the county and settled his case favorably. While the police did not admit any fault, the government paid Hernandez $7,000 for the unearned jail time and to help compensate him for losing his new job. What they didn't do, however, was fix the computer database. On March 15, 1988, the L.A.-based Hernandez was pulled over again, this time because his vehicle registration had expired. Once again, his name came up in the crime database: He had an unpaid ticket for failing to wear a seat belt, and again, an outstanding warrant for his arrest issued by the Chicago PD. This time he was jailed for seven days, but his employer didn't fire him.

BONUS FACT

In the late 1990s into the early 2000s, it was not uncommon for Major League Baseball prospects from outside the United States to adopt false identities to appear younger (ultimately helping them make more money as professional athletes). Perhaps the best example is Fausto Carmona, who debuted with the Cleveland Indians in 2006, claiming to be born in December 1983. According to *The Plain Dealer* of Cleveland, "officials in the US and Dominican Republic were tipped of [Carmona's] true identity by a woman who claimed she doctored a false birth certificate." Carmona was really born in 1980. His real name? Roberto Hernandez.

BROASTER PRINCE VERSUS BURGER KING

The Other Ronald McDonald

There are well over 10,000 McDonald's franchises in the United States as of 2019. And by and large, when one McDonald's restaurant opens, it stays open; the fast-food giant has proven quite popular, becoming a mainstay in most communities. There are some exceptions, however—for example in 1996, when the lone McDonald's franchise in the small Illinois town of Fairbury (population 3,200 or so), lost out to Ronald McDonald. No, not the red-headed clown who first appeared in McDonald's marketing in 1963. Unfortunately he was late to the game in Fairbury because by the time he became the mascot of the burger giant, Fairbury's own Ronald McDonald—let's call him Ron, for simplicity's sake—was in his mid-twenties.

Ron McDonald was born around 1940, to Earl and Dorothy McDonald. In 1956, his parents opened up a family-style restaurant on the main strip in town. Featuring Midwestern fare such as "broasted" chicken (chicken that is fried in a pressure cooker), the eatery quickly became a favorite hangout for Fairbury's residents. The name? McDonald's Family Restaurant. At the time, the McDonald's corporation didn't care, in part because the corporation itself barely existed; Ray Kroc, the entrepreneur often credited with making the burger chain into the behemoth it is today, didn't buy into the company until 1955.

In 1970, however, McDonald's finally took note of—and aim at—McDonald's Family Restaurant. That year, Ron told the *Chicago Tribune*, McDonald's sent his parents the first of many letters filled with ominous legal language. "It warned us about ever using arches or going to a drive-in format, and it kind of scared my folks, but they didn't think there was anything they could do about it," said Ron. But the real battle began in 1992, when the McDonald's corporation opened a franchise in Fairbury. More legal wrangling ensued; Ron told the local press that "[McDonald's] had a team of lawyers come down and practically insist we (change the name) but we said no, we can't do that." Ron and his wife Sue did make one concession, however: They dropped the possessive "s" from their restaurant's name. Even that didn't matter, though; as the Associated Press reported, "locals just called the family-owned place 'McDonald's East' and the fast-food joint, 'McDonald's West.'"

Ultimately, residents ran the burger king out of town. It wasn't out of animosity, just disinterest; per a corporate spokesperson, "McDonald's West" closed in 1996 because "there really weren't enough sales generated." Ron McDonald offered a similar explanation, noting that "there are a lot of retired people in town....They don't patronize fast-food places much." In the small town of Fairbury, Illinois, there was only enough room for one Ronald McDonald, and the red-haired clown lost out. With this exit, the legal threats also ended. As a result, the couple re-added the possessive "s" to their establishment's name. It would remain there for another twenty years until the couple retired in 2016, shuttering the restaurant.

BONUS FACT

There is no Ronald McDonald at Japan's McDonald's franchise. Instead, the mascot is named "Donarudo Makudonarudo," or "Donald McDonald," as it's easier for native Japanese speakers to pronounce.

THERE'S NO PLACE LIKE MCDONALD'S

The People Who Live Under the Golden Arches

As of 2019, Hong Kong is home to more than seven million people and is one of the wealthiest places in the world. If it were a country in its own right, the autonomous city would rank within the top ten in per capita GDP (gross domestic product). But there's another side to the city's economy, however: rampant poverty. According to a Bloomberg report, just over 20 percent of the nation was living in poverty in 2018. Additionally, many of these less fortunate residents are homeless—and the problem has only gotten worse. According to a *South China Morning Post* report, homelessness in Hong Kong tripled between 2006 and 2016 (to about 1,600 people total).

For those without a place to sleep, affordable late-night accommodations can be hard to come by. Fortunately in Hong Kong, there are more than one hundred free options—if you don't mind the smell of hamburgers, that is. This is because approximately half of the 253 McDonald's restaurants in Hong Kong are open around the clock. As a result, many of Hong Kong's impoverished citizens make their way to the nearest franchise—not for a meal, but for a good night's sleep. As the BBC reported, "as night falls, the fast-food restaurant becomes a temporary hostel, attracting dozens of the city's poorest people." In the US, those nonpaying customers would typically be asked to leave, but in Hong Kong, the opposite is true: McDonald's Hong Kong has reported that they "welcome all walks of life to visit our restaurants any time" and aim to be "'accommodating and caring' to customers who stay a long time in restaurants 'for their own respective reasons.'"

Of course, there are some limits to such accommodations. In late 2015, for example, a fifty-six-year-old woman went to sleep one night at a Hong Kong McDonald's and the next day was discovered to have died overnight. Fortunately, this kind of tragedy is rare; for many sleepers, the open-door policy of Hong Kong's burger joints has created a sense of community where there is typically isolation and squalor. The company and spaciousness of this temporary lodging is a welcome sight—even to those who are not homeless. One such man who has a tiny apartment near the McDonald's franchise that he often sleeps at told the BBC that the restaurant "is a familiar place, with familiar faces. These people are all wanderers. Some come for a short while, others a long time. Most of them don't have a home. They have nowhere else to go."

Unfortunately, Hong Kong's homeless problem has gotten worse over the years since. According to a 2018 report in the *South China Morning Post*, "the number of registered homeless people in Hong Kong has jumped almost 22 percent in the past year as sky-high rents force the city's poorest inhabitants to sleep rough," either on the street or taking shelter at fast-food restaurants.

BONUS FACT

Hong Kong borders China and is technically part of China, but if you drive from one to the other, you're going to need a visa—and a separate GPS system. Most of the world uses something called "WGS-84" as the basis for the digital maps. China, however, uses something called "GCJ-02." Digital maps in China, therefore, don't match the digital maps used by Hong Kong or the rest of the planet. China isn't just trying to be different, though; the government has long seen map data as a matter of national security and thus greatly restricts the creation and use of digital maps in the region.

DEAR LEADER, THANKS FOR THE FRUIT

China's Temporary Love Affair with the Mango

Mangoes are indigenous to South Asia, with about 40 percent of the world's mango production coming from India. While the fruit isn't native to China, it has become quite popular there; about 10 percent of all mangoes are grown in this region. And for a while, mangoes were more than just a cash crop for China: They were a symbol of patriotism.

Back when Mao Zedong ruled the country, a lucky loyalist may have received a mango that was meant as a keepsake, not as a snack. In one example, the fruit was placed in a glass case adorned with an inscription like, "Respect and Wishes to Chairman Mao for a Long Life, Commemorate Great Leader Chairman Mao who gave this cherished gift—Mango—to Capital Worker-Peasant Mao Zedong Thought Propaganda Team." The case usually also had an image of Mao on it. The entire contraption, called a "mango reliquary," was a shrine to the mango.

So how did this mango "worship" begin? In 1966, Mao began his Cultural Revolution: a purge of the non-Communist aspects of Chinese society. This required an army of sorts, of course, so he tapped into the youth of the nation—students—and created the Red Guards, a paramilitary group whose members were often blindly loyal to Mao. But that loyalty was often subject to interpretation, which resulted in chaos and violence. Inspired by Mao's often vague pronouncements, they made dedicated efforts to figure out exactly what the statements meant; factions quickly formed based on the different interpretations of Mao's statements. While all of these groups pledged their complete loyalty to Mao, they frequently engaged in verbal and physical fights with one another throughout the Revolution. Mao needed a way to stop this factionalization, so, per *Slate*, he "asked 30,000 Beijing factory workers to act as peacekeepers." These factory workers called themselves "The Worker-Peasant Mao Zedong Thought Propaganda Teams." Many died in this effort, but they were ultimately successful in keeping the peace between factions.

Just prior to one of the team's major victories, Mao met with diplomats from Pakistan (one place where mangoes originally came from). The diplomats gifted Mao a crate of about forty mangoes, which he in turn regifted to the Thought Propaganda Teams—likely not thinking much of it. The workers thought otherwise. As art historian Freda Murck told the BBC, "No one in northern China at that point knew what mangoes were. So the workers stayed up all night looking at them, smelling them, caressing them, wondering what this magical fruit was." To them, the mangoes weren't a snack or dessert: They were exalted to the level of something worthy of worship. The forty mangoes were sealed in wax cases called "mango reliquaries" and put on display in factories throughout the region as a symbol of the workers' value in the eyes of their Chairman.

From there, the mania quickly spread. As *The Telegraph* explained, "plastic, wax, and papier-mâché facsimile mangoes were sent out on special lorries to tour the provinces, while enamel mugs, washbasins, and plates were decorated with mangoes. Fake mangoes in glass cases were handed out to thousands of workers in Beijing." Ultimately, however, the mango madness was (for reasons unclear) short-lived. About a year or two after the original gift from Mao, the fruit's cultural luster lost its significance—leaving a lot of odd relics behind.

BONUS FACT

Harvesting mangoes comes at a cost: itchiness. One of the natural oils found in the mango tree contains a compound called urushiol, which is the same allergen found in poison ivy, poison sumac, and poison oak. The allergen is also in the fruit's skin, but not the fruit itself, so eating peeled mangoes won't cause irritation.

WAX IN, WAX OUT

The City Where It Pays to Stick Things in People's Ears

As of 2019, the Chinese city of Chengdu is home more than ten million people (nearly twice that amount if you include its greater metro area). As one would expect from a city of this size, it's a major economic center; more than half of the *Fortune* 500 have a footprint here, and its airport is one of the world's fifty busiest. But Chengdu also knows how to take a break. If you walk through the streets of the city, you'll almost certainly notice how many teahouses and bars there are. They are so common, in fact, that in 2006, the *Los Angeles Times* dubbed Chengdu "China's party city."

If you stop off for some tea at one of Chengdu's many options, you may also find yourself stepping into another sector of the city's economy—one which you won't find anywhere else in the world. For the equivalent of about $1.50 (USD, as of 2019), someone may offer to clean out your ears. If you live in Europe or the Americas, this will probably come as quite the surprise; in general, wax extractions in these regions take place in the comfort—or at least privacy—of one's own home. However, in the streets of Chengdu, ear wax removal is a very public affair: a strange mix of hygiene and performance art. The entire process takes anywhere from twenty to thirty minutes, not including the few minutes spent haggling over the price.

In 2002, a reporter with the *San Francisco Chronicle* described her experience with this "art": "[The ear cleaner] uses an eight-instrument technique. First he runs a thin file along the ear lobe and outer edges of the ear canal to remove hair. Next he uses a thinner file, a flexible metal strip, to gently loosen the wax. Larger pieces of wax that come loose easily are removed with a pair of pincers. Smaller particles are scraped out by a bamboo stick with a small scoop at the end." After the wax is removed, the cleaner finishes up by sticking "a bamboo stick with down feathers," into the ear. Finally, a "tuning fork is gently snapped against the stick, causing the feathers to vibrate inside the ear canal." It's kind of like a massage, but performed inside one's ear.

If this seems like something that shouldn't be done by an amateur, don't worry: It isn't. The process to become an ear cleaner in Chengdu is long, often involving two years of study, and cleaners are expected to perform seemingly superhuman tasks to become official. Per the BBC, "one such exercise has them using tweezers to pluck tiny threads out of a lit candle wick without extinguishing the flame." That said, it's unclear if there's any sort of licensing system that can help customers know if the person has gone through this training. As for the ear cleaners themselves, though, the time invested in studying and steadying their hands is often well worth it. Per the *Chronicle*, a Chengdu ear cleaner can earn north of $300 (in US currency) in one month. That's about $3,600 per year in a place where the average annual income is less than $1,000.

All humans have ear wax, but not all of have the same *type* of ear wax. If you're a native English speaker, you almost certainly have wet, amber- to brown-colored ear wax (an estimated 97 percent of people of European and African descent have this type). If your family comes from East Asia, however, there's a good chance you have dry, gray, and flaky ear wax (an estimated 30–50 percent of the population has this type). Because of these differences, ear wax is useful for anthropologists: It can help them determine a person's ancestry.

BLUE EAR

The Superhero with a Single Purpose

Mosaic trisomy 22 is the name of a chromosomal disorder in which some of the person's cells have a third (and therefore extra) copy of chromosome 22. Mosaic trisomy 22 affects one in four thousand people, and those with the disorder have varying degrees of developmental problems, including heart defects and cognitive disabilities. As in the specific case of a young boy named Anthony Smith from Salem, New Hampshire, Mosaic trisomy 22 can also cause severe hearing loss. Anthony has no hearing in his right ear, and minimal hearing in his left ear that requires the use of a blue hearing aid. However, back in 2012 at around the age of four, he refused to wear it. His reason? As he told his mom, "superheroes don't wear blue ears," and therefore, neither would he. His mom was at a loss for what she could do. This sounded like a job for a superhero—or at least for Marvel Comics, the major comic book franchise that created heroes such as Spider-Man, Captain America, and Iron Man.

After Anthony's complaint, his mother, Christina D'Allesandro, emailed Marvel hoping for assistance in convincing her son to wear his aid. She feared that the email would not get past Marvel's spam filters (as a statement by the company warned), however, so she certainly did not expect the response she received. In a surprising twist of events, the comic book giant created a poster for Anthony. It featured a superhero known as the Blue Ear, who was named after Anthony's hearing aid. The Blue Ear wore a listening device (just like Anthony) that gave him the ability to hear cries for help and respond in a timely, super fashion.

By all accounts, Marvel's idea worked. Anthony not only began wearing the hearing aid again but also started carrying the pinups of the Blue Ear around with him to school (and virtually everywhere else). His preschool became quite keen on the superhero as well. In fact, administrators loved the idea so much that, according to Fox News, they instituted a "dress up like a superhero day." Not only did this allow all of the students to become superheroes for the day, but it also gave Anthony the chance to emulate the character that he inspired. He could turn into the Blue Ear, wearing his aid proudly for all of his classmates to see.

Marvel was not done there, though; in March 2013, the comic book company teamed up with hearing aid distributor Phonak to create a public service announcement that featured popular superhero Iron Man. In the announcement, Iron Man encouraged children to be tolerant and understanding of the unique needs of children like Anthony, and also demonstrated the ways that technology can improve lives (like with Anthony's hearing aid). As for the Blue Ear himself? He won't be appearing in any actual Marvel comics, but that's okay: His work here is done.

Iron Man's true identity is Tony Stark, an industrialist who sold weapons to the US military during the Vietnam War era. Why was this the chosen backstory? When Stan Lee created Iron Man in 1963, the United States was increasingly anti-war and skeptical of those who profited from their business dealings with the military. Lee wanted to see if he "could take the kind of character that nobody would like...and shove him down their throats and make them like him." Suffice to say Stark has won over quite a few people across not just America, but the world.

AIR PLANE

The Invisible Wonder Woman Toy Everyone Wanted

Wonder Woman first graced the comic book industry in December 1941, when she appeared in DC Comic's *All Star Comics*, Issue 8. Since then, she's become arguably the most recognizable, beloved female superhero in not just the US but the rest of the world as well. Aside from having super strength, she's armed with indestructible bracelets, a boomeranging tiara, and of course, her Lasso of Truth—a rope that, when it ensnares a bad guy (or for that matter, a good guy), prevents him from telling a lie. But perhaps her coolest gadget isn't one she's always equipped with—or for that matter, one she's ever been seen with: the Invisible Jet.

The Invisible Jet wasn't just a method of super transportation in the Wonder Woman comics: It was a symbol (albeit a hard to see one). According to the *DC Comics Encyclopedia*, the jet was originally a social commentary on the "invisible" compliance expected of women when they were forced into the labor pool during the Great Depression. The plane moved quickly and went undetected, all while doing the job it was tasked with; similarly, women of the era were expected to avoid conflict wherever possible, instead focusing solely on getting their work done.

As the years ticked by, however, this allegory was lost. And perhaps coincidentally, the Invisible Jet became less and less important in the Wonder Woman storyline. By 2010, it was something of a joke. Actually, that's an understatement: By 2010, it was *literally* a joke. That is until it became real (though still invisible). In July 2010, San Diego hosted the forty-third annual Comic-Con, a gathering of comic book fans and those who worked in the industry. Mattel, the toy licensee of Wonder Woman (and other DC Comics characters), decided to use her phantom plane as a promotional tool at the event. A few months before Comic-Con, they announced a new product on their *Facebook* page: a collectable Invisible Jet action figure.

Most fans immediately saw through the scheme: The date of the *Facebook* announcement was April 1, and the Invisible Jet was actually an April Fool's joke. Some people weren't willing to see the truth, however. Despite the fact that there wasn't anything to it, die-hard fans wanted the collectable "plane," and asked Mattel how to get one. Mattel seized the opportunity; as the *Los Angeles Times* reported, "so many people asked the company where they could purchase the item that Mattel decided to make it a limited-edition collectible." Mattel ended up making the Invisible Jet available for $5 as an exclusive item sold only at the 2010 Comic-Con. The "toy" was just packaging; the plastic mold inside the case contained an outline of a plane, to help sell the joke. And it sold pretty well, despite the empty packaging. Today, the not-quite-real Invisible Jet is sought-after by collectors, and has fetched over $100.

Wonder Woman's Invisible Jet is a lightning rod for April Fools' jokes, it seems. On April 1, 2013, Seattle's Museum of Flight announced that the jet would be available for a limited, three-day engagement in its halls. The plane's entry on their website noted that the plane was ahead of its time: Its "technology demonstrated advanced stealth and speed capabilities more than twenty years before comparable human-built aircraft." The museum has since removed the page from its website, but if you think about it, you're really not missing out on anything.

HEADLESS POTATO

The "Bring Your Own Potato" Toy

On May 1, 1952, the Hassenfeld Brothers toy company—later re-named Hasbro Inc.—brought to market the original Mr. Potato Head toy. At 98 cents each, the toy was instantly popular, selling over one million units in its first year. A far cry from the toy you see on the market today (and the beloved character in the *Toy Story* films), this original version had a key thing missing: the potato head.

That's right: The original Mr. Potato Head (designed in 1949 by inventor George Lerner) was headless. Packaged into a box called the "Mr. Potato Head Funny Face Kit," the toy was merely a collection of parts: goofy eyes, protruding ears, a huge nose, a pipe, and of course, a mustache. Children were intended to apply the parts to a real potato (no, it wasn't included in the kit)—or any other vegetable or fruit of their choosing. Another early version of the toy even sold these parts piecemeal, as inserts in cereal boxes.

So why the change to the plastic potato head? No, it wasn't for convenience or to reduce the mess that parents had to clean up: It was the government. In 1964, new regulations from the government required that certain safety guidelines be met in all products intended for use by children. Unfortunately for Hassenfeld Brothers, the parts included in the original Mr. Potato Head

Funny Face Kit proved too sharp to meet these regulations. The manufacturers rounded the points of the insertion pegs on each part, but in doing so, made it too difficult for kids (or even adults) to stick the parts into real fruits and vegetables. As a work-around, Hassenfeld Brothers came up with a plastic toy head.

In 1975, manufactures doubled the size of the head and accessories, again to meet new regulations and also to market to younger children. A compartment was also added to later versions so children could store the parts inside the head. With these improvements, Mr. Potato Head became the toy you are familiar with today. Since then, he has permeated popular culture—not only in the *Toy Story* films but also in his own TV show and in a variety of commercials. He even received four votes in the 1985 mayoral run in Boise, Idaho (an uncontested Guinness World Record). And in 1987, he set down his original pipe accessory for good in order to help the American Cancer Society promote its efforts to end tobacco use.

You'll find Mr. Potato Head's full story at the National Toy Hall of Fame in Rochester, New York. And if you are interested in collecting all of his fun, limited edition accessories, you'll find everything from Santa Claus hats and chef aprons to vampire fangs and guitars. There is even a Mrs. Potato Head (also shown in the *Toy Story* films), as well as potato pets (affectionately known as "Spudettes"). Needless to say, this potato isn't going anywhere anytime soon—and unlike the original, he comes with all parts included.

BONUS FACT

Mr. Potato Head was the first toy to be advertised on TV in 1952. It was also the first time an advertisement specifically targeted children. Many manufactures would soon follow suit; in 2007, it was reported that $17 billion was spent on advertising to kids in the US that year.

NOT THE TOYS YOU'RE LOOKING FOR

The Empty Box Christmas That Kids Loved

Star Wars: A New Hope debuted in movie theaters on May 25, 1977, and took the world by storm shortly thereafter. Today, the galaxy far, far away is everywhere: movie sequels and prequels, books, TV shows, and of course, toys. Merchandising is where the real money from the Star Wars movies is made, after all. At least, that was the bet Star Wars creator George Lucas placed when he made the first movie. As *The Hollywood Reporter* explained, 20th Century Fox, the movie studio behind Star Wars, "let Lucas pass up an additional $500,000 directing fee in return for keeping licensing and merchandising rights for himself." As a result, Lucas made billions. But not immediately. No one—well, no one except George Lucas—expected the movie to be the smash hit it was.

When it came to making Star Wars toys, this lack of foresight proved to be a problem. Per *Den of Geek*, "action figures take a long time to produce. They have to be designed and sculpted. Those sculptures have to be turned into steel molds. The toys then have to be cast, painted, and safety tested. Then they have to be packaged up and shipped off to toy stores." That often takes a full year, and in the case of *Star Wars: A New Hope*, there wasn't enough time to get toys onto store shelves. As a result, the demand was intense and the supply virtually nonexistent. For about $10, the film producers sold those seemingly unpromising rights to Lucas.

Kenner, the Star Wars toy licensee at the time, knew that action figures would be a top seller. They also knew that the earliest they could get the products to market was February 1978, which would be well after Christmas of the year Star Wars was released. Their solution: The Star Wars Early Bird Certificate Package. Accounting for inflation, this $10 package cost about $40 in 2019—so it was hardly cheap. And you didn't get much for that investment: some stickers, a sheet of cardboard with a display stand that featured action figures (that didn't yet exist) resembling characters from the movie, and a Star Wars Space Club membership card.

There were no toys in the package—nothing whatsoever to actually play with. Those, the Early Bird package promised, would come later. Each package also contained a postcard for kids to fill out with their name and address. They'd mail it into Kenner, and sometime between February and June 1978, Kenner would send back a set of four action figures: Luke Skywalker, Princess Leia, R2-D2, and Chewbacca. It was the best that Lucas and Kenner could do to get something on shelves before Christmas.

The media had a field day with what they perceived to be incompetence, calling the product an "empty box" that children would immediately find disappointing. However, many parents of Star Wars–crazed kids disagreed; Kenner made hundreds of thousands of the Early Bird packages—and they sold out. The next spring, children across America celebrated part of their Christmas a little bit later. For them, it was an experience that was worth the wait.

In 1987, Mel Brooks released *Spaceballs*, a movie parodying Star Wars. In the movie, Yogurt (his answer to Yoda) proudly shows off a line of *Spaceballs*-licensed products while declaring that "merchandising is where the real money from the movie is made!" Yet, if you were a kid looking for *Spaceballs* action figures, you were out of luck; Brooks received Lucas's permission to produce the Star Wars spoof, but Lucas requested that Brooks not allow for *Spaceballs* action figures, as they'd look too close to the legitimate Star Wars ones. Ignoring Yogurt's advice, Brooks agreed.

YOU BETTER NOT SHOUT, I'M TELLING YOU WHY

How the US Military Brings Santa Claus to Faraway Towns

Micronesia is a collection of thousands of islands and atolls in the Pacific. Many of the islands are inhabited, although few have sizable populations; Guam, a US territory since the close of the Spanish-American War, is the most populous, with roughly 160,000 citizens. Some of the islands have formed a nation called the Federated States of Micronesia, which has just over 100,000 citizens spread across it. Of these citizens, about 500 live on an atoll known as Kapingamarangi, which is a roughly one square kilometer ring of land encapsulating seventy-five square kilometers of what would otherwise be ocean.

Kapingamarangi is not the type of place the US military would typically bother with, especially not during the relatively peaceful year of 1952. However, late that winter, a Boeing B-29 Superfortress—a strategic bomber used against Japan during World War II—was flying above the area. The locals gathered on the atoll's beaches and started making hand gestures at the plane, which was flying low enough to notice what the people were doing. In response, the bomber's crewmen dropped their payload onto the beaches below. No, they didn't drop bombs, nor were the hand gestures from the Kapingamarangi locals lewd or otherwise unwelcoming (they were actually waving hello to the plane). As Senior Chairman Carlin Leslie described in an article on the *Pacific Air Forces* website, when the crew saw the "islanders waving to them, [they] quickly gathered some items they had on the plane, placed them in a container with a parachute attached, and dropped the cargo as they circled back." The crew scattered what else they could find onboard across a handful of other inhabited islands in the region as well, and because of the time of year, this impromptu humanitarian mission became known as Operation Christmas Drop.

Each year since, the US Air Force has repeated the operation, making it the longest ongoing defense mission. In recent years, residents of Guam have also joined the efforts, donating food, clothing, household goods, toys, school supplies, and fishing nets. These items are gathered into boxes weighing roughly 400 pounds each. The Air Force then outfits the hefty "care packages" and drops them just offshore throughout Micronesian islands (ensuring that no one gets hit by a nearly quarter-ton crate from the sky).

For many recipients, this influx of goods is critical. Few of the islands in the area have an airstrip, and it's hard to dock a cargo ship on a ring of sand. As a result, these islands are isolated from the rest of the world, with no effective means of importing stuff. The Operation Christmas Drop gifts are one of the few ways that new wares enter their local economies. As one Air Force member told the military press, Operation Christmas Drop "is a yearlong wait for these items, and for most of us it's the only way to obtain new clothes and Christmas gifts." As a bonus, the operation also "serves as a training mission" for the flight crew. And besides, it's fun to be Santa.

BONUS FACT

Spam—the canned meat product, not the annoying email—is really popular in Guam. According to the official Spam website, the average Guam resident eats sixteen cans of it each year. In Hawaii, you can even get Spam at McDonald's—it truly is a Pacific favorite!

IT WAS A WONDERFUL LIFE... EVENTUALLY

How a Commercial Failure Became a Holiday Classic

Frank Capra is one of the most decorated directors in American history, with six Academy Awards and nine other nominations to his name. He's perhaps best known for *It's a Wonderful Life*, which led to Academy Award nominations for both Best Picture and Best Director in 1947 (the winners were *The Best Years of Our Lives* and William Wyler, though Capra did win Best Director for the film at the Golden Globe Awards that year). This Christmastime classic follows George Bailey, played by James Stewart, as a guardian angel tries to convince him not to take his own life. But you probably knew that already; the film is seen by millions of viewers each year, and for many families has become part and parcel of their winter traditions. By that measure, *It's a Wonderful Life* was a smashing success. However, in order to get there, the film had to first be a box office failure.

In 1945, Capra and a few others founded Liberty Films, an independent movie studio with Capra at the helm. They were well funded, with about $1 million in cash, and a credit line of $3.5 million at their fingertips (accounting for inflation, that's well north of $50 million in 2019). In December 1946, *It's a Wonderful Life* became the first movie Liberty Films released. With a production budget of over $2.3 million, the film needed to make more than twice that at the box office to break even. Unfortunately it didn't come close. Despite the all-star cast and crew, critical acclaim, and Oscar nominations, *It's a Wonderful Life* didn't do so…well, wonderfully, in its initial release. It ultimately eked out about $3.3 million.

While not a total disaster, the film's lack of success put Liberty Film's financial future (and the future of its distribution partner, RKO Radio Pictures) in jeopardy. Hoping to avoid bankruptcy, Capra and his team agreed to sell the studio to Paramount Pictures in 1947, just months after *It's a Wonderful Life* was initially released. The film became the property of Paramount in the deal, and over the years, ownership of the film rights bounced around from one company to another—each trying to figure out a way to make money off this good but commercially unsuccessful film.

In 1974, something happened that solved their problem—or, more correctly, nothing happened. As movie website *Screen Rant* explained, the copyright law at the time required the holder to renew every twenty-eight years. National Telefilm Associates (NTA) owned the rights to *It's a Wonderful Life* at the time, but for reasons unclear, they did not file for renewal. As a result, the movie entered the public domain, meaning anyone could air it without paying royalties. And many, many TV stations did exactly that. The movie aired repeatedly during the Christmas season, becoming a viewing tradition for many households. NTA's successor entity, Republic Pictures, was able to effectively reclaim the copyright in the mid-1990s, but by then the movie had been a regular on American TVs for decades, entering the pantheon of must-watch movies of the holiday season.

BONUS FACT

Another bump in the road for *It's a Wonderful Life* came from law enforcement—specifically, the FBI. According to *Philadelphia* magazine, J. Edgar Hoover (the Bureau's long-time director) issued a memo warning people to stay away from the Christmas classic. As Hoover wrote, the movie "represented rather obvious attempts to discredit bankers by casting Lionel Barrymore as a 'scrooge-type' so that he would be the most hated man in the picture" (a tactic he claimed was "a common trick used by Communists").

AND THE OSCAR DOESN'T GO TO...

The Most Famous Man in Hollywood You'll Never Get to Meet

In 1969, the movie *Death of a Gunfighter* debuted. Starring Richard Widmark and Lena Horn, it received a mixed response, viewed as mediocre at worst—"extraordinary" at best; *IMDb* gives it a viewer-powered 6.4 stars out of 10, while Roger Ebert gave it 3.5 stars out of 4. Ebert made special mention of *Gunfighter*'s director in his review, writing, "Director Allen Smithee, a name I'm not familiar with, allows his story to unfold naturally. He never preaches, and he never lingers on the obvious. His characters do what they have to do. Patch gradually gets in deeper and deeper. There's another killing. The county sheriff is called in. The town council finds its self-respect threatened by this man who will not bend. The film ends in an inevitable escalation of violence, and in a last sequence of scenes that develops with horrifying understatement." *The New York Times* also noted in its own review that the film was "sharply directed by Allen Smithee who has an adroit facility for scanning faces and extracting sharp background detail."

This was high praise for the director; there was only one problem: Allen Smithee isn't real. During the making of *Gunfighter*, the actual director (Robert Totten) and lead actor (Widmark) had what you might call "creative differences." In the middle of the shoot, Widmark successfully stumped for Totten's removal, and he was replaced in the director's chair by Don Siegel. Siegel did not want to take credit for directing the film, having worked on less than half of it and, in his eyes, being something of a yes-man to Widmark (Siegel believed Widmark was the de facto director). Totten, for his part, also refused to take credit for a film he was cast off from. The Directors Guild of America (DGA) agreed, and instead associated the film with a made-up director, "Al Smith"—a name quickly revised to "Allen Smithee" in order to avoid confusion with real people of that common name.

The DGA continued to use the name (more commonly spelled Alan Smithee) officially through 2000, in order to disassociate directors and films whenever a situation called for it. Most of the situations involved movies you probably haven't heard of as they didn't turn out all that well, but Alan Smithee also has credits in some well-known TV shows. He's officially the director of an episode of both *The Twilight Zone* and *The Cosby Show*, as well as two episodes of *MacGyver* (including the ninety-minute pilot). Whether it was poor ratings or creative differences between the director and other members of the cast and crew, the Smithee name gave directors a way to disassociate with work that they didn't think was up to their standards.

Credit for the ultimate retirement of the Smithee name went to another movie: *Burn Hollywood Burn*. In the film, the protagonist is a director named Alan Smithee. The movie was a critical failure and subsequently received a lot of negative press. With the "Alan Smithee" name now a punch line, the DGA believed the moniker had outlasted its value, so they stopped using it. But don't worry: A director can still disassociate from a film if circumstances warrant doing so. The DGA is more than willing to use other pseudonyms, deciding on a case-by-case basis.

BONUS FACT

Edward Norton earned an Academy Award nomination for Best Actor for his role in *American History X* in 1998. The movie's director, Tony Kaye, was unhappy with the film, however, and specifically with Norton's alleged re-editing of the movie to give himself more screen time. Kaye requested that the DGA credit him as "Alan Smithee," but the DGA refused, as directors were prohibited from revealing to the public why they requested the Smithee treatment. Kaye ended up suing the DGA and the studio (New Line Cinema) for more than $200 million, and requested that if he couldn't use "Alan Smithee," he be credited as "Humpty Dumpty," a request that was also rejected.

OSCAR DE LA RENTAL

The Award Even Money Can't Buy

In 2013, Daniel Day-Lewis became the first person to win the Academy Award for Best Actor three times. He joined Katharine Hepburn, Ingrid Bergman, Jack Nicholson, Walter Brennan, and Meryl Streep as the only actors to date to take home three (or more in Hepburn's case: She won four) of the coveted Oscar statuettes. Unfortunately, he or his heirs may have to return these little golden men one day—if they try to sell them, that is.

Each year, the Academy of Motion Picture Arts and Sciences (AMPAS) gives out the Oscar statuettes—officially called the Academy Award of Merit—in a variety of categories (twenty-four total, as of 2019). AMPAS has been giving out Oscar statuettes since 1929, and while there are not a lot of them in circulation, there are certainly enough for a shrewd collector to find someone willing to sell one. In fact, there have been many instances of such sales, as evidenced by the fair number of Oscars in the hands of nonwinners. For example, magician David Copperfield reportedly purchased the 1943 Best Director Oscar (awarded to Michael Curtiz for *Casablanca*) for nearly a quarter of a million dollars. The award was later placed up for auction by a subsequent owner, at a price of nearly $3 million.

AMPAS, most likely in an effort to keep the winners' circle (and accompanying statuette) exclusive, has since put a wrench in such transactions, however. As of 1950, Academy Award winners must agree to give AMPAS first right of refusal if the honoree (or his or her heirs) ever try to sell their Oscar(s) to a third party. If they do so agree, AMPAS's repurchase price is $1 (yes, one measly dollar). And if the honoree refuses to sign this contract, AMPAS similarly refuses to give them the Oscar they earned.

Enforcement of the clause is not unheard of, either. As *Quartz* reported, actress Mary Pickford won an Oscar in 1929 and another (honorary one) in 1975. The 1929 award was not encumbered by the clause, but the 1975 one was. When her heirs tried to sell the former, AMPAS argued—successfully—that when Pickford accepted the latter statuette, she agreed retroactively to bind her first award to the $1 terms as well. The jury ultimately decided that the terms of the agreement applied to her heirs, and the judge blocked the sale. On the other hand, CNN has reported that in 2011, Orson Welles's heirs put his 1941 award for Best Original Screenplay on the auction block. AMPAS couldn't prevent *this* sale, as Welles hadn't signed the (at that time nonexistent) agreement.

Whether the clause should be enforced is certainly a matter of debate, and practically speaking, enforcement is a difficult call to order regardless. *Forbes* estimates that roughly 150 Oscars have been sold since AMPAS began awarding them in 1929, and about half of them are "gray-market sales involving post 1950-statuettes."

BONUS FACT

In 1939, Walt Disney received an honorary Academy Award for *Snow White and the Seven Dwarfs*; the achievement "recognized as a significant screen innovation which has charmed millions and pioneered a great new entertainment field for the motion picture cartoon." The award wasn't the standard statuette, though: It was comprised of eight statuettes in total—one standard-sized statuette placed atop a stepped base, with seven smaller ones on tiny steps leading up to the standard one.

A KERNEL OF HISTORY

The Story of Movie Theater Popcorn

Movies and popcorn go hand-in-hand. If you shell out the $13 (okay, more like $15 in 2019) for a ticket, you're probably not going to balk at a medium popcorn for $4.75. After all, it's something that Americans have done for generations—although it doesn't necessarily make sense. People can certainly go two to three hours without eating, and even if they did need sustenance more often, the empty calories plus salt and fake butter in movie theater popcorn aren't exactly going to meet nutritional needs.

During the film, the crunching noises as your neighbor munches away can be distracting, and at the end of the film, there's almost always a good amount of popcorn and other sticky messes on the floor. So, why do Americans continue the tradition? More specifically, whose idea was it to sell popcorn in movie theaters?

Movie theaters themselves have been around since the early 1900s; one of the first dates back to 1905. That year, a pair of entrepreneurs in Pittsburgh opened what was known as a "nickelodeon": A storefront theater that played silent movies on a continuous loop. For one nickel, patrons could watch for as long as they wanted. The business proved popular, spreading throughout the United States. Ultimately, however, nickelodeons were too successful for their own good. As a trip to the movies became more and more popular, these small theaters needed to expand. Unable to do so, they were replaced by large venues.

For the next decade or two following this change, the new movie theaters saw themselves in competition with live theater, so if you went to one of these early movie theaters, you'd be in for a fancy experience. As *The New York Times* reported, "after you bought a ticket, you might pass through gilded archways and ascend a grand staircase lighted by a crystal chandelier to find your velvet seat." It was more like a visit to a modern opera than to the next Avengers movie. And just like the opera, popcorn wasn't welcome within.

By then, though, popcorn had become a popular street food. In 1885, a Chicago inventor named Charles Cretors developed a way to pop kernels using steam and without the need of a kitchen. Street vendors subsequently popped up in many urban areas, including near movie theaters. Much like today, some theatergoers at the time would buy a snack on the street in hopes of sneaking it into the movies. Of course, the theaters discouraged this behavior; per *Smithsonian*, "early movie theaters literally had signs hung outside their coatrooms, requesting that patrons check their popcorn with their coats."

In 1929, though, this changed. The Great Depression gripped American society, and like everyone else, movie theaters were feeling the pinch of lower demand. Unless they modified their business models, they'd be at risk of bankruptcy. So instead of preventing patrons from sneaking popcorn into the movies, many theaters partnered with popcorn vendors to provide snacks for their guests. Yes, that meant the velvet seats would end up getting messy, but it was better than the alternative. As *Smithsonian* explained: "A Dallas movie theater chain installed popcorn machines in eighty theaters, but refused to install machines in their five best theaters, which they considered too high-class to sell popcorn. In two years, the theaters with popcorn saw their profits soar; the five theaters without popcorn watched their profits go into the red." Popcorn allowed the movie theaters to survive.

BONUS FACT

Popcorn kernels pop in two different types of shapes: "butterflies," which flare out in two directions like butterfly wings; and "mushrooms," which are shaped like mushrooms. If you're eating pre-packaged, prepopped popcorn at home, you're most likely eating mushroom-shaped kernels, as they tend to be more resilient. Movie theater popcorn comes in both shapes.

AT LEAST THE POPCORN IS FREE

Inside the Movie Theater Chain for the Rich and Famous

In general, the movie-watching experience at home is pretty good; there is a huge library of content available, from *iTunes* and *Netflix*, to cable TV and DVDs. There are also really big TVs, impressive sound systems, and comfortable seating on the market. And while this experience doesn't quite replicate that of a movie theater, there are other advantages: The bathrooms are clean, the snacks are healthier, the floors aren't sticky, and the only cell phones ringing are your own. The dream of the perfect in-home movie experience *is* missing one key ingredient, though: Today's latest hits aren't immediately available. Most movies aren't released for home viewing until weeks if not months after they hit theaters. Unless you're rich and connected, of course.

Back in the 1920s, some of Hollywood's elite figured that there had to be a better way—so they made one for themselves. It started informally when a handful of movie moguls head-lined by producer Louis B. Mayer (of Metro-Goldwyn-Mayer fame) got together and formed a club of sorts. Each member built a small movie theater in his or her own home—screens, a projector, etc.—most likely to view older movies whenever they wanted to anyway. But having an in-home theater proved more valuable than they originally thought. This small cadre of movie moguls now had access to new releases from each other's studios, and through their informal arrangement, could review these films in the privacy of their homes.

Over time, their clique grew; if you knew someone, you, too, could join what was dubbed the "Bel Air Circuit." You would need to have enough money to build your own studio, hire a projectionist, etc., but really, it came down to connections—one couldn't just buy her or his way in. As the decades ticked by, the Circuit became more and more formal. In late 2017, *HuffPost* described the privileges of membership: "Wanna catch up on Academy Award-nominated movies…? Hollywood insiders historically can get the movies on DVD even if they aren't out on home video. Now, with a Bel Air Circuit screening room, these insiders get the movie the way the director intended it for their consideration right in your home."

In recent years, Hollywood—in search of new income streams—has found ways to give people who aren't part of the Bel Air Circuit access to a similar experience; all you need is a big enough checking account. In 2010, *The Wrap* reported that if you knew the right people, you could buy your way in through a rumored initiation fee of $100,000 up front and then $4,000 a month—plus the cost of creating a home movie theater worthy of inclusion in the club. And in 2015, *The Verge* reported on a company that provided Circuit-like access at a reduced rate; $35,000 up front would get you a device that let you rent out movies the day they come out in theaters, plus an additional $500 per movie.

But don't expect this service to be available at a cheaper price anytime soon: Hollywood is still very protective of the box office revenue. The security around the $35,000 device shows just how serious they are. According to *The Verge*, "only authorized users can rent a movie, which requires that they swipe their thumbprint across the futuristic, angular security terminal...the box is also equipped with accelerometers and will stop working if it's moved." And if you get around that? "An invisible watermark on every movie identifies which box is in use. That way...an owner can be identified."

BONUS FACT

The list of Bel Air Circuit members isn't publicly available, so it's unclear whether Will Smith is on it. However, when his TV show, *The Fresh Prince of Bel-Air,* debuted in 1990, he almost certainly was not: He was on the verge of bankruptcy. Despite having a successful rap career before the show aired, Smith (per CNBC) "was living beyond his means and not paying his taxes." Smith needed a payday. Per the *Hollywood Reporter*, his then-girlfriend "suggested [he] just hang around Paramount...in hopes of meeting someone influential." It worked: He met a TV executive who introduced him to entertainment legend, and future *Fresh Prince* executive producer, Quincy Jones.

ADMIT FOUR

The Road to Zyzzyx Road

If you're making a movie, the goal probably isn't just art: You want to make money too. Typically, you do so at the box office by selling tickets for the film, but there are other ways to do so as well, such as selling DVDs and distributing the film internationally. If you can keep production costs down, your movie can make money even if it doesn't do well in domestic theaters—which is why it was totally okay that a 2006 movie titled *Zyzzyx Road* made only $20 from ticket sales in its domestic release. (No, not $20 million, or even $20,000. $20 total.)

The movie itself is a typical thriller. The protagonist, a man named Grant (played by Leo Grillo), is a husband and father on a business trip in Vegas. While there, he meets Marissa (Katherine Heigl). The two go back to a motel room and, while getting intimate, are surprised by Marissa's ex-boyfriend, Joey (Tom Sizemore). Joey attacks Grant, but Grant strikes back and accidentally kills Joey. At first unsure of what to do, Grant tosses Joey's body into the trunk of his car and drives away to bury it.

However, when he arrives in the middle of nowhere—Zyzzyx Road—Joey's body isn't in the trunk anymore. Joey isn't dead! (Cue gasps from the audience.)

As movies go, it is formulaic but not terrible, sporting a 4.6 (out of 10) star rating on *IMDb*. A low score, sure, but hardly the worst: There are dozens of movies with ratings lower than 2 stars. So why did it do so poorly at the box office? That was by design. Grillo, who was also the movie's executive producer, wanted to be able to pay the movie's stars (all members of the Screen Actors Guild) a lower-than-standard rate. Screen Actors Guild (SAG) rules allow lower-budget films (like *Zyzzyx Road*, which had a budget of only $1.25 million) to do this, as long as the movie had a domestic theatrical run.

The cost-conscious Grillo didn't want to invest a lot of money in this SAG-required run, of course, so he paid a small Dallas theater $1,000 to screen the movie once a day, every day, for one week (specifically at noon) to fulfill his obligation. Grillo and his team did not expect *anyone* to show up at the theater, but six people did. That is, six people total showed up to watch the film over the seven-day run, spending $5 apiece. Two of the paying viewers were a makeup artist who worked on the movie and her friend, so Grillo returned their money, and the movie unofficially grossed $20 at the box office. $1.25 million spent (including $1,000 to the Dallas theater), with $20 in revenue—it was not exactly a box office smash. But don't weep too much for Grillo and *Zyzzyx Road*: As noted, this was all part of the plan. It worked, and Grillo was able to pay the actors less than the standard rate.

Unfortunately for Grillo, his hopes for a payday from international theaters and domestic at-home (e.g., DVD and on-demand) viewing didn't pan out. All told, the movie earned about $400,000 (plus the $20 from the Dallas theater) by the end of 2006.

BONUS FACT

It's rare to find things that are spelled with a double "Z"—but you can find one in the Rock and Roll Hall of Fame. The band ZZ Top was inaugurated into the Hall of Fame in 2004. And the trio isn't only known for their music: They're also known for their facial hair. The lead guitar player and vocalist, Billy Gibbons, and the bassist and other vocalist, Dusty Hill, sport long, bushy beards. The only member of the band who sometimes goes clean-shaven is the drummer. His name? Frank Beard.

CATCHING UP ON YOUR Zs

When Getting the Spelling Right
Was a Bridge Too Far

Starting in November 1964, if you wanted to drive between the New York City borough of Staten Island and the borough of Brooklyn, you had to take the Verrazano-Narrows Bridge. Named for Italian explorer Giovanni da Verrazzano, the bridge has since lent its name to the community. Today, there are dozens of businesses and even a public school in the area that bear the name "Verrazano."

If you're a copy editor (or otherwise invested in the use of correct grammar), the previous paragraph probably bothers you quite a bit. Exactly *how* many Zs does the bridge have in its name? Well, that depends on who you ask—and when.

The naming of the bridge was controversial from the get-go. During the planning phase, the bridge was to be named the "Narrows Bridge," after the body of water it spans. However, Italian-American heritage groups lobbied for naming the bridge after Verrazzano, as they wanted a way to anchor the importance of Italian contributions to New York. They ultimately made headway, winning over Governor W. Averell Harriman in 1958.

Opponents of the name change decided to redirect their argument to the spelling—specifically, the number of Zs. According to the *New York Post*, the bridge was to be named "Verrazano" with one Z "because of a typo in an original construction contract." Those who wanted to honor the Italian-American community lobbied to fix this error, and at first, it seemed like they would succeed. At a ceremony in New York City, Harriman announced that the bridge would in fact be named for the explorer, spelled with two Zs. Mayor Robert F. Wagner Jr. then declared that day be named "Verrazzano Day" (again two Zs). The headline of *The New York Times* article about the event rang out: "Verrazzano Gets His Day and his 'Z.'"

That pronouncement was premature, however: The great "Z" debate was far from finished. The bridge was years from completion, and the one-Z side kept up the fight. It turns out that their efforts weren't just based on a "typo," either; the true spelling of the name was ambiguous. While some sources, such as *Encyclopedia Britannica*, spelled the explorer's name with two Zs, others, such as the *Columbia Encyclopedia*, listed it with one.

When Harriman left office at the end of 1958, each camp lobbied the new governor, Nelson Rockefeller, to use the number of Zs they preferred. In April 1959, Rockefeller decided on one Z; per a *Times* report, he believed that was the "accepted American spelling" of the Italian explorer's name.

And yet, the debate *still* didn't end there. In August of that year, Rockefeller and others took a ferry boat to Staten Island for the groundbreaking ceremony, only to discover that the boat itself was also named for the explorer—and it was spelled with two Zs. As the state legislature had not yet passed a law naming the bridge, the debate was briefly rekindled. Ultimately, in March 1960, Rockefeller signed into law a bill that named the bridge the Verrazano-Narrows Bridge—with one Z.

Today, the bridge still services commuters to and from Staten Island, but it's no longer the "Verrazano." While decades passed, the spelling still didn't sit well with Italian Americans. In 2016, an online petition demanding that "the bridge be renamed with the correct spelling of the explorer's name" received a good deal of press coverage, which in turn led to legislative action. In October 2018, the bridge finally got its second Z.

BONUS FACT

Despite the bridges connecting Staten Island to New York and New Jersey, there is one group that prefers a different route across the water: deer. According to the *Staten Island Advance*, there were only about two dozen deer living on Staten Island in 2006. By 2017, however, that number exploded, reaching approximately two thousand. How did the deer get there? Some were born from those original twenty-four or so, of course, but most commuted from New Jersey in search of food or new habitats. They didn't take a bridge, though: They swam.

Z

A DECLARATION OF INDEPENDENZE

The Battle of Zee versus Zed

Z. It's the last letter of the English alphabet, no matter where you live or what dialect you speak. However, when it comes to what you call it—well, that depends. If you speak American English, it's pronounced "zee." If you speak British English, it's pronounced "zed." And if it seems like an odd thing to differ on, that's probably the point.

The letter Z has been pronounced "zed" for a very long time. It gets its name from the Greek letter Z (uppercase) or ζ (lowercase), pronounced "zeta." That's why the Spanish call Z "zeta," the Germans pronounce it "zet," and the French say "zède": It all goes back to the Greeks. All except for "zee," that is. The first recorded use of the "zee" pronunciation comes from a 1677 treatise called "New Spelling Book." It listed "zee" as one of many acceptable pronunciations, along with "izzard," "ezod," and other options that weren't used very often. At the time, it seemed that "zee" would similarly vanish from the English lexicon; "zed" still ruled the roost.

A full century later, though, something happened: War broke out in the New World. The British colonies revolted against the Crown and won. America was born. And for the generations that followed, finding ways to become more and more independent from Great Britain proved popular. Enter Noah Webster, an early American politician and lexicographer; known today for the series of dictionaries that bear his name, he was a man with a love for language—and a disdain for the British. So he combined the two passions.

In 1828, at the age of seventy, Webster published his first edition of the *American Dictionary of the English Language*. It was the most comprehensive effort of the time: seventy thousand words, of which nearly 20 percent had never been listed in a dictionary before. One of his major goals with this dictionary was to simplify the language by showing a preference for spellings that matched how words were pronounced. For example, both "center" and "centre" were acceptable spellings; Webster adopted the former as the official version, as it matched how the word is actually said.

Simplification wasn't Webster's only motive, however. He also wanted to further establish American independence—linguistically speaking, at least. In 1755, British lexicographer Samuel Johnson had published *A Dictionary of the English Language*, which established norms throughout the British Empire. His treatise preferred spellings that connected words to their etymologies, favoring, for example, "colour" over "color." Webster chose spellings that broke away from this European model. He did the same for pronunciations, as well; the entry for "Z" in his 1828 dictionary ends with the simple, authoritative claim that "it is pronounced zee." Webster's dictionary, in no small part due to its break from the Crown's English, established itself as the definitive source for the English language in America; with that, Z in the United States became "zee."

BONUS FACT

One of Noah Webster's other notable changes was to drop the "-ue" at the end of words such as "catalogue." If you look up the word "tongue" in his dictionary, you won't find it; Webster listed it under the spelling "tung" and stated that "our common orthography [that is, 'tongue'] is incorrect." Suffice it to say, his spelling didn't stick.

BORN IN JULY...OR AUGUST?

Why Americans (Kinda Sorta)
Get Independence Day Wrong

"In Congress, July 4, 1776," begins the Declaration of Independence, "the unanimous declaration of the thirteen united States of America." From this document came the birth of the United States, and from that came Independence Day. This day is celebrated annually in the United States on the fourth of July, but some believe that July 4, 1776, is not truly America's day of independence. That honor, they claim, should fall to either July 2, 1776, or August 2, 1776.

On June 11, 1776, the Continental Congress created a committee of five delegates—Thomas Jefferson, John Adams, Benjamin Franklin, Roger R. Livingston, and Roger Sherman—empowered to write a first draft of a declaration of independence. Jefferson took the lead, and the quintet delivered their draft on June 28. After a few days of debates and revisions, Congress officially voted to declare independence—on July 2. The next day, Adams wrote a letter to his wife, Abigail, discussing the Declaration and its significance. He explained: "The Second Day of July 1776, will be the most memorable Epocha, in the History of America. I am apt to believe that it will be celebrated, by succeeding Generations, as the great anniversary Festival. It ought to be commemorated, as the Day of Deliverance by solemn Acts of Devotion to God Almighty. It ought to be solemnized with Pomp and Parade, with Shews, Games, Sports, Guns, Bells, Bonfires and Illuminations from one End of this Continent to the other from this Time forward forever more."

While Adams appropriately described the revelry, he whiffed on the date. Though there would be an annual celebration thereafter to commemorate the birth of the nation, it wouldn't be on the 2nd of July, it would be on the 4th. And while the date *is* significant in American history, it was not the day the Declaration of Independence was signed, as many believe; it was the day the Continental Congress ratified the text of the document. Ratifying the text simply meant that it was confirmed, not that it was made official law. The signatures needed to make it a true law had yet to come.

According to *National Geographic*, many of those who would sign the famous piece of parchment were not present on the 4th of July when it was ratified, so it was not fully signed until August 2. This belief is also buttressed by the journals of the Continental Congress itself, as stated by the National Archives, "on August 2, the journal of the Continental Congress records that 'The declaration of independence being engrossed and compared at the table was signed.'" One of the most widely held misconceptions about the Declaration is that it was signed on July 4, 1776, by all the delegates in attendance.

While the July 4 date is probably the least relevant of the three, it would later lend itself to a fantastic coincidence. Of the five drafters of the Declaration, Adams and Jefferson went on to become Presidents of the United States. And Adams and Jefferson share something else in common, as well: Both died on July 4, 1826—fifty years to the day the Declaration was ratified.

BONUS FACT

July 2 is a special day for another reason: In non-leap years, it is the midpoint of the year (there are 182 days before it and 182 days after it). This was not true the year the Declaration was signed, because it was a leap year.

FEBRUARY 30

The Time Sweden Messed Up the Calendar

"Thirty days has September, April, June, and November." This little rhyme is a common way to remember the length of each month; those four have thirty days, and the others have thirty-one. The exception, of course, is February, which usually has twenty-eight days. Every four years, however (unless the year is divisible by 100 and not divisible by 400), an extra day is added to the calendar. That extra day is February 29, which bumps March 1 forward to the next day. Under no circumstance is there ever a February 30—unless you were in Sweden or Finland in 1712.

Up until the late 1500s, Europe and North Africa used the Julian calendar, a 365.25-day calendar originally promulgated by Julius Caesar. The Julian calendar did not account for the fact that the Earth actually takes a bit less than 365.25 days to revolve around the Sun, however, so after the first few dozen centuries of use it no longer synced with the seasons. This fact was of particular concern to Pope Gregory XIII, as Easter was supposed to loosely coincide with the spring equinox but no longer did. In 1582, he fixed this issue by promulgating the Gregorian calendar, which had fewer leap years than the Julian.

Most Catholic nations enacted the new calendar by jumping from October 4, 1582, (on the Julian calendar) to October 15, 1582, (on the Gregorian) the very next day. This meant that, in those nations, October 5–14, 1582, never existed.

Not all countries followed suit so quickly, however. Of particular note was the Swedish Empire (which includes modern-day Finland), which decided not to adopt the new calendar at first. Then, in the late 1600s, they thought better of this decision, believing it was time to join the rest of the world. Yet even with this decision, they were in no rush. Instead of dropping eleven days off of their calendar all at once, they decided to simply ignore all leap years from 1700 until 1740, thereby losing the eleven days over a period of four decades. On March 1, 1740, Swedish calendars would sync perfectly with those using the Gregorian calendar.

Unfortunately, this plan went awry. For some reason, the empire forgot to skip the leap years in both 1704 and 1708. They had managed to drop only one day in eight years, and, even worse, were now no longer aligned with other holdouts still using the Julian calendar. In 1712, the king came up with a solution; instead of simply dropping ten more days and joining the Gregorian nations, he instead rejoined the Julian ones. In 1712, the empire had two leap days: One as usual, and one to make up for the lost day in 1700. The second leap day? As seen in the Swedish almanac from that year, it was February 30.

BONUS FACT

May 35 also doesn't exist—for most people, anyway. In China, this date is used online to discuss the Tiananmen Square incident, which occurred on June 4, 1989. As noted by *The New York Times*, Chinese censors often filter out the date "June 4," so many use "May 35" as a work-around—at least until the censors catch up.

THE METRIC SYSTEM VERSUS TIME

A Failed Attempt to Create a Ten-Hour Day

There are sixty seconds in a minute, sixty minutes in an hour, and twenty-four hours in a day. You probably knew that already, but only because you've committed it to memory—it's not something you can reason out. In fact, it's not entirely clear to *anyone* why days have two twelve-hour halves, or why hours have sixty minutes made up of sixty seconds each. Per *Scientific American*, the ancient Egyptians are possibly the culprit: "The importance of the number twelve is typically attributed either to the fact that it equals the number of lunar cycles in a year or the number of finger joints on each hand (three in each of the four fingers, excluding the thumb), making it possible to count to twelve with the thumb." It could also be thanks to the ancient Babylonians, who used a base-sixty system. Of course, neither of these civilizations are around today—so, why hasn't the world switched to decimal time?

If the French Revolution is any indication, it's because the average person doesn't really care about the math behind the clock. Starting in the 1750s, philosophers and mathematicians began to write about their struggles with both the base-twelve system for time and the system used for weights and measures—to them these seemed counterintuitive or, at least, antiquated. When the French revolted against the monarchy forty or so years later, the political upheaval spread beyond politics and into this realm; after the storming of the Bastille, the French nobility made many concessions to the revolutionary forces, including relinquishing control over the official weights and measures. This became the first major step toward the modern metric system, which France adopted in 1837.

But the revolutionaries weren't only concerned with pounds and inches; they also tried to reform the minutes and hours, too, using something now called "French Revolutionary Time." The idea was simple: ten-hour days, with each hour consisting of one hundred minutes, and each minute consisting of one hundred seconds. On November 24, 1793, this base-ten system became the law of the land, and clockmakers began to produce clocks with two rings— one showing the time using the old way and another that showed it the new way. The changes didn't stop there, either. Gone were seven-day weeks: They were replaced by ten-day weeks. Each month was now thirty days, each made up of three weeks. There were still twelve months, in order to make the math work, but each month was renamed to reflect the seasons in Paris. Five celebratory days (six in leap years) came at the end of the year.

At least, that was what the law said. In practice, people didn't really care to change how they kept time. As *Mental Floss* explained, unlike weights and measures, which impacted trade and commerce, "there were few practical reasons for nonmathematicians to change how they told time." The base-twelve system was good enough— plus, replacing clocks meant spending money. Failing to get the people on board, the government ultimately gave up their attempts to change time. All in all, the experiment lasted less than eighteen months; by spring of 1795, the French leadership dropped the edict.

BONUS FACT

The Babylonians' base-sixty system probably had a practical reason behind it. The number sixty is the lowest number that has the numbers one–six as factors, allowing for an easy and equal division among different measurements.

TIME TO GO TO JAIL

When Connecticut Criminalized Daylight Saving Time

Daylight Saving Time (DST) is controversial. People debate whether changing clocks twice annually is a good idea, and similarly, they quibble over whether Daylight Saving Time is better than Standard Time. One aspect should be uncontroversial, however: Communities should pick one together and apply it across the board. After all, if the school bus driver thinks it's 7 a.m. but the principal thinks it's 8 a.m., that's a problem. For the sake of everyone's sanity, when it comes to deciding what time it is, people need to find a way to get along...even if it means putting people who disagree in jail.

The jail part seems a bit extreme, actually, but it's what the state of Connecticut once thought. In 1922, the state's legislature—controlled by farmers who wished to have consistent time year-round (and didn't mind having an earlier sunrise and sunset)—really didn't like Daylight Saving Time. In response, they did what legislatures do: They passed a law requiring that the entire state remain on Standard Time year-round. The law was ineffective, however, as it didn't have any penalties associated with it, and a few of the state's mayors decided to "spring forward" anyway.

As *Time* magazine reported, "the cities used Daylight Saving Time, while the executive and judicial departments of the state and the railroads kept their clocks at Standard Time but moved their schedules an hour ahead."

The legislators were none too happy about this "illegal activity." Per *Time*, one legislator "offered a bill to provide four commissioners at salaries of $10,000 a year [a six-figure job today, adjusted for inflation] to go about the streets, examine the watches of citizens and take those to jail who used Daylight Saving Time." The rest of his lawmaking colleagues didn't have the intestinal fortitude to incarcerate those who dared change their watches, so the bill failed. No one became a criminal for adjusting his or her watch—at least, not right away.

A year later, the resolve of the anti-DST crowd proved stronger. In 1923, the state passed a law which, per *Time*, "[forbid] the 'willful display in any public building, street, avenue, or public highway of any time-measuring instrument or device, which is calculated or intended to furnish time to the general public, set or running so as to indicate any other than the standard time." And this law had teeth; a violation meant you were subject to a $100 fine (about $1,400 in 2019)—or up to ten days in prison. Despite this, some people still decided to switch their clocks. As ConnecticutHistory.org recounts, a Hartford jeweler, in a direct affront to the law, "[set] the clock in front of his jewelry store ahead one hour." His case made its way to the Connecticut Supreme Court, which ruled that the criminal penalties for violating the statute were perfectly constitutional. In Connecticut, observing Daylight Saving Time was truly against the law.

Fortunately, Connecticut changed course in the 1930s, and Daylight Saving Time became okay once again. Today, the entire state changes its clocks twice a year—and does so without risking a prison sentence.

BONUS FACT

Daylight Saving Time may be hazardous to your health—or, at least, the spring time change can be. According to a 2014 article published in the *Open Heart* journal, "the Monday following spring time changes is associated with a 24 percent increase in [heart attacks], and the Tuesday following fall changes is conversely associated with a 21 percent reduction."

ABOUT THE AUTHOR

Dan Lewis is a father, husband, Mets fan, lawyer, and trivia buff. He writes a daily email newsletter called "Now I Know," which began in June of 2010 with twenty subscribers and now boasts more than 125,000. A proud graduate of Tufts University and the Benjamin N. Cardozo School of Law, he's currently a digital strategist for a well-known children's company. You can sign up for his newsletter at NowIKnow.com.

NOW YOU CAN
KNOW IT ALL!

PICK UP OR DOWNLOAD YOUR COPIES TODAY!

adamsmedia
An Imprint of Simon & Schuster
A CBS COMPANY